Time to

It was the end of a terrible season for Frampton Athletic
Rangers we had been relegated, the atmosphere around the club
was nonexistent, and to be honest Saturdays had not been
enjoyable for a while. It was time for a change, and with me
being too young to take up golf there was only one option… I
was going to stop playing Football and play Rugby.

Having played Rugby whilst growing up, mainly for school
with a few games for Clifton Colts and the odd game for the
Bristol schools combination, I was by no means new to the
sport, I just hadn't experienced being a member of a "proper"
Rugby club and playing senior Rugby. But who should I play
for?

As far as I was aware I had 3 options:

I could go and join the club I played a few games of Colt's
Rugby for at Clifton, however the standard was high, my name
wasn't Tarquin, I didn't shop in Waitrose, or own a Pony, and I
wasn't 43rd in line to the throne;

I could follow a few lads from school and go to play for
Aretians who I had played the odd youth game for, though this
was not within walking distance of where I lived and would
reduce the possibility of staying for a beer;

Or

I could play for my local team, Frampton RFC. It was close to
home, I knew a few of the players and although when growing
up Frampton didn't posses a good junior team at my age level
(in fact they were shit) from what I had seen on the odd

occasion, the senior team looked to know what they were doing.

During the summer of decisions I was regularly visiting the local gym in a bid to keep myself fit and put a bit of meat on the bones. I was your typical lanky teenager at this point having not done any weight training before. I could run for miles, I just wasn't sure I was ready for running with 17stone men trying to crush me.

It was at the gym I bumped in to one of the Slate twins – it's not that I can't tell them apart as one is more portly than the other - I just can't remember which one it was. Now both of the Slate twins who were two years older than me and were some of the Rugby "stars" at school had been playing for Frampton since they were twinkles in their Mother's eye, or close to it. They lived next to the hallowed turf, their Dad had been captain of the first team and they even thought it was cool to wear the Frampton shirt to school when they hit sixth form. Basically they loved Frampton. Knowing this information it was no surprise to me that when I mentioned to him that I was looking for a club to play for, he suggested without hesitation that I should join Frampton (or Fram, as it was soon to become affectionately known) and that pre-season training would start the first week in July.

My decision to play Rugby instead of Football was met with mixed reactions:

Dad – "about bloody time"

Mum – "don't end up with a back like your Dad's"

Granddad – "That will be good"

Girlfriend - "Why? Isn't that dangerous. You shouldn't do that. You can't stay out long mind, what time will you be home. Don't go on any tours!"

Football manager – "Why didn't you give me more notice, I would have gone out to look for a centre half... you were in my long term plans" (Where this professionalism came from I'm really not sure).

However only 2 of these were of any importance, Dad's and Granddad's; they were the ones that were going to be stood on the sideline in the Forest of Dean on a cold Saturday afternoon in January.

My Dad gave me my earliest memories of Rugby, going to watch him play for Avon & Somerset Police on a Saturday afternoon. I remember the smell of deep heat, an orange at half time and then going home to watch the A-Team in the evening. It was safe to say that having previously played Football with my old man, he was a Rugby player pretending to play Football rather than someone who could actually play Football. This could also be said for his Cricketing abilities. Don't get me wrong he could definitely play but his mantra was hit it/them and hit it/them hard. Finesse was not a word he associated with sport.

You might think that playing for the Police they would be a fair bunch that were always on the right side of the laws of the game with no skulduggery going on at all. If you do think this you are gravely mistaken and only have to look at ex England players to realise this - none more so than Wade Dooley and Paul Ackford, England's towering second rows. Another way to see this wasn't the case and a way that was far more interesting was to look at my Grandmas old newspaper cuttings of when my Dad was playing. There were the obvious ones where he scored a hat trick, kicked 20 points or won the cup; however, these were nowhere near as intriguing as the cuttings where he had been sent off for fighting and the one where he was sent off for kicking. He still pleads innocence to this day... well kind of, "I honestly didn't kick him! I punched him".

My Dad was proud and excited when I told him in my first year at school that I had made the Year 7 A team. I remember him being less than convinced however when I told him I was playing second row - "that's no place for you, you get out of there and score some tries". Unfortunately when I joined school I was tall, and this coupled with the fact my first PE teacher knew nothing about Rugby meant by default I was in the engine room.

Luckily for my looks and my Rugby career my playing days in the second row were very short lived and after proving that as well as being tall I was fast, could catch, pass and put in the occasional tackle I was soon selected in the centre. A much safer place. This all coupled with the fact I had ears that would rival Gary Linekar and Prince Charlie also meant the second row was no place for me.

School Rugby had its highs and lows over the years, all of the highs coming from when the first inept PE teacher left the school and was replaced with a teacher whose main sport was Rugby rather than Polo. Not surprisingly all of the lows came in the earlier days of school life when no one really had a clue what we were supposed to be doing, and the PE teacher had even less of a clue (maybe there was a correlation)!

One such occasion was when we travelled down the M5 to play a strong Clevedon side. I realised on this trip that Rugby teams are not always blessed with the most intellectual of players when our flanker asked as we crossed the Avonmouth Bridge "are we in Wales?" I don't think he sat Geography in his exams.

The game started brightly with the sun being out. Apart from that it was bleak. They ran in tries at will, luckily for me now in the backs, the majority came from a beast of a number 8 called Huw Bennett, who was to go on to wear the number 2 jersey for Wales. I honestly believe he was the same size then as he is now. I was just very thankful I had managed to get out of the Second Row before that game came around.

As always my Dad and Granddad had come to watch the match, and I remember on the way home my Dad asking who the pillock was that was shouting random instructions to us in the first half but then spent the second half watching the hockey match going on 100 yards away. (The aforementioned PE teacher!)

Whilst playing for the school I was selected for the Bristol Combination team with a good mate of mine Ed. Ed played his Rugby outside of school for Bristol and was ever prominent in the front row. Now Ed wasn't your typical front row in that he giggled, a lot, and to make it even worse he giggled at such a pitch that only dogs could hear him. In fact if you couldn't see Ed and heard him laugh you may think that he was a six-year-old girl.

Our first game for the Combination was away against Rhwbina School in the Welsh valleys on a cold and wet Wednesday night in November. We boarded the coach in Bristol and took our seats. I didn't know anyone on the coach apart from Ed. Ed however knew a large contingent of the team from playing for Bristol. As the coach journey got underway, the usual banter started with various members of the team being singled out for their fair share.

We then got on to the subject of Football as there were International matches taking place that evening. Someone on the back seat piped up and asked, "who are England playing tonight?" To which I replied "the Netherlands". Now my front row friend Ed had been quiet on the coach so far, and he should have stayed quiet as after my response he replied as quick as a flash with "No it's not the Netherlands Mike, its Holland!" As you can imagine the remainder of the coach journey was focused on Ed and his excellent geographical knowledge. The other members of the front row union were not impressed as it only confirmed what most of us already suspected. However Ed did go on to obtain an A level in Geography - and they say exams aren't getting easier!

All of my Rugby to this point had been played on School pitches or at local council owned parks. Playing Rugby in Wales however was different. The coach drove through a small Welsh town (later on in life I would discover it was Pontypridd) and the parked in a stadium. First of all I was amazed that we were playing in such a place for a School combination game and secondly I couldn't believe that a town this size actually had a stadium! As we entered the gates I remember seeing a sign above us that read "House of Pain". Now I knew there was a rivalry with the Welsh but putting up a sign was a bit much!!!

The sign could not have been more accurate. We were absolutely destroyed, beaten up and pummelled into the ground by the best youth team I had ever played against. My over riding memory is of their number 8 running the length of the pitch flattening everyone that got in his way and scoring what was his umpteenth try that game. His name was Gareth Delve, another future Welsh international I had the unpleasure of playing against!

One of the high points in school Rugby was when we were entered into the inaugural 7s tournament at Rosslyn Park. Not only was it a trip to London instead of normal lessons we would also be pitched against some of the top schools in the country. Looking at our fixtures for the tournament we had been drawn against Harrow. They were bound to boast some talent, and if they didn't then surely they would have been coached to be able to beat a school from South Gloucestershire. Especially when their master was ex England coach Roger Utley!! What on earth had we let ourselves in for?

We kicked off, and in usual 7s style we kicked long to try and peg them back in their half. Unfortunately we kicked to their South African flyer who proceeded to dance round all seven of us, put on the after burners and score in the corner: 5-0 down, 15 seconds gone!

What then proceeded was as close to forward dominating Rugby as 7s could be, as we decided the only was to beat the public school boys was to literally beat them. And that we did, led by our ginger animal Tom Bass we ground out a 12-5 win that the whole school could be proud of. Unfortunately we were stuffed in the next round but hey-ho we had a moment to savour.

After this came my first taste of cup success in Rugby. The School first team had made its way to the regional cup final to be played at Clifton, a ground where I had played a few times before (more on that later). It would be mine and a few other lads' last game playing in the school colours and this of course meant two things: we had to win, and we had to somehow keep some kit for keepsake.

The school first team possessed a fair amount of talent and aside from good school players we had Dave Ward at flanker who was an absolute animal around the park. (Dave would go on and transform himself into a top class Hooker playing for sides such as Bath, Sale and Harlequins.) And we had Ollie, a mercurial Fly Half who had a spell at Colton's on a scholarship, was as quick as a winger and had a kick like a mule.

The final as a game was a non-contest; we ran out easy winners, so easy I can't remember the score. What I do recall was a number of schoolmates making the trip over to Clifton to watch us, and the fact that this would be the first time my girlfriend would have watched me play (she did try to make the semi final but arrived after the final whistle) so I was also keen to impress. After ten minutes into the game I thought I had done just that; I managed to score the opening try of the game, result! After the match, obviously excited having just lifted the cup I asked my girlfriend if she had seen my try…."Did you score, I arrived 15 minutes late". There was a theme developing and needless to say it continued during our relationship!

Whilst playing Rugby at School I did begin to think that maybe I should start playing for a club outside. As aforementioned Frampton was not an option given how bad they were, a couple of lads at school played for Bristol (this sounds better than it was as back then anyone could play, although they were very good) but for some strange reason I found myself playing Colt Rugby at Clifton. Probably due to the fact that my Dad used to work with the coach down there, a big Scottish bloke by the name of Bill McGrath.

Playing at Clifton was an odd experience, the side was mainly made of up boys from Bristol Grammar School, Colton's and Queen Elizabeth Hospital, with the exception of myself, Bill's boy Craig (who had Scottish junior caps – another monster), and Dave the Mexican who was a good mate of mine at the Ridings.

Given that I was very much an outsider in the team of Hooray Henrys, I just tended to go with the flow. This did however mean that on some match days when the regular backline was available I was asked to play in the pack, luckily not in the second row but on one of the flanks, and again I think this was due to me being tall!

Apart from my brief stint of one game at second row I had avoided the pack like the plague so had no real clue of what my job as flanker was to entail apart from being part of the scrum and lineout. And what I was to do there I had no idea, and to be honest, I still don't have much of a clue! I just figured I would run around, stand by the side of rucks, make the odd tackle, join the back of the mauls, stand at the back of the lineout and not get involved, do something very similar in the scrum with a token bind and when I had ball in hand play as if I was in the backs…I was wrong.
During the warm up of the first match I was to play flanker I was told I would be jumping in the lineout and my first thought was how hard could it be! All I have to do is jump at the right time, and remember the calls that the halfwits in the forwards remember (some of the time)…again I was wrong.

After being told the calls I was ready to put this jumping lark in to practice, "blue 32, 24 with a camel", and up I jumped. Now as any good lineout jumper will know you should jump straight up and keep your legs together but, as I was not a good line out jumper I jumped as high as I could not taking into account any technique and ended up kicking one of my lifters in the crown jewels and almost landing on the other on the way down! Not a good start.

After a brief bit of coaching I was ready to go again, and this time it was a success: I jumped up, was held there for a few seconds, caught the ball and back down. Easy. In fact it was so easy for the lifters it prompted them giving one of the more regular jumpers a load of stick for being how they eloquently put it - a "fat b*st*rd".

Now that the lineout was mastered it was on to the scrum, and here my prediction of how I would make an impact was correct, -I wouldn't. I would make a token bind, not bother to push and wait for it all to finish. Simple.

Luckily for me playing Rugby as a flanker for Clifton turned out to not be too dissimilar as playing in the Centre; mainly because we were so dominant all positions seemed to merge into one, except for when there was a set piece. However I was still sure that the pack was no place for me.

Playing for Clifton I obtained my first proper injury playing Rugby,. Now what I want to say is that I put in a huge tackle and smashed my shoulder... or that I was concussed by stopping a twenty stone prop; however, it was nowhere near as exciting and no one else but myself was involved!

We were defending a twenty two metre drop out and I was on the line watching the "funny", as their Fly Half kicked the ball I jumped up to block the kick, got nowhere near it and then when I landed turned over on my ankle. I had never been the most graceful person, and balance and fleet of foot were not skills I possessed in my locker. As a result of my inability to jump up and land properly I had ankle ligament damage and therefore no sport for 3 months. B*ll*cks!

Cheers Shag

It was the first Tuesday in July and that meant it was time for pre season training to start, and for me to begin my time with Frampton Rugby club. I was excited about joining a Rugby club but also nervous. Would I be good enough for senior Rugby? Was I fit enough? Strong enough? And most worryingly of all would I be able to tackle an eighteen stone Neanderthal running at me?

Luckily I would not have to answer all of my questions at the first training session. Frampton's home pitch was Crossbow House (Stade de Frampton) and somewhere I was very familiar with having played all my youth Football there, and frequented on a Friday night when we were too young for pubs.

I arrived at Crossbow on a warm, sunny Tuesday evening and there were already a few players running around playing touch. (By 'touch' I mean touch Rugby, not the game that was played in schools around the world where you were safe if you were off ground.) I headed for the changing rooms where I was met by the one of the Slate twins (again I can't remember which one). He seemed fairly happy that I had turned up so I took that as a positive and headed outside for training.

Touch Rugby was a perfect way to start, however it's one of the Rugby games that unlike the full version of the game doesn't suit all shapes and sizes. Thinking about it playing touch Rugby at the start of training or to warm up before a match may just have been a way to wind up and anger the forwards. Anyway I joined in, and everything seemed to be going quite well and I even managed to score a try by sprinting round my opposite man - this pre-season Rugby lark was easy!

The coach of Frampton Rugby club back then was Simon Brooks (Brooker). A small man, with the syndrome associated with small men. Si had represented Frampton in their back line in years gone by and was still more than able to hold his own on the training pitch. I was introduced to Brooker who asked where I played and who I had previously played for. I'm not sure Frampton Rangers Football club was the answer he was hoping for, however I think he was slightly hopeful in the fact I brought the average age of the people training down quite significantly.

As was expected with pre-season training it was time to sweat out the Summer's indulgence, and by the look of some players the Summer had lasted a lot longer than normal! Fitness training for pre-season 12 years ago was pretty basic compared to where we are now as back then it consisted of lots of shuttles with plenty of press ups thrown in - equally painful just not as productive in terms of fitness results. Yet just as productive in terms of making people throw up, leave early, develop an "injury" and for those that had earned the right just to point blank refuse (this was usually reserved for the front row prop who had been with the club for donkeys years, or as he was known in this club, Zaff -more about him later).

Pre-season and fitness sessions never bothered or worried me back when I was younger, and this probably helped me impress more than I actually should have done during my first training session. In all of the runs I was up there with those out in front, and didn't really complain or look like I was going to have a cardiac arrest after it. Although as with anything, fitness is relative, and whereas before playing Football I was training with people that were all of a similar disposition, this was certainly not the case with Rugby.

In the bar after I was introduced to a few more members of the club - Mike Weaver (Weaves), Cornish (or Dave of Cornwall as he calls himself), Tony Williams (Shag), Badger and the first team captain at the time Paul Beet, who at no point should you call Beety, but you could also call Shag! Paul was an ex Para and straightaway I realised that he was someone that you wanted on your side!

Pre-season began to become much more serious and physical the closer we got to the start of the season, with more of the training involving splitting forwards and backs, and running through specific moves: the backs with their lines of attack and the forwards practicing their scrums and lineouts.

All of the back's moves were being orchestrated by Fly Half Weaves, and seemed to be fairly similar with different variations on 3 or 4 basic lines of running. I remember back then the moves were T1, T2, M1, M2 and then the very exotic M1 double loop. Again times have changed and so have the moves, and even if some stay the same there are definitely different calls, for example "magic", "piss off" and "animal ball". Playing in the centre meant that I had to learn all the moves quickly as one way or another I was involved either being a dummy runner or a dummy actually receiving the ball.

In all the Rugby I had played before there were never really any "moves" - it was more a case of once you caught the ball you had 3 options, pass, kick or run! In fact playing for the school I generally had one option –run. My fellow centre was a Footballer who was being made to play and he used to tell me before every game "I don't want the ball, and I'm definitely not tackling" and he was right, he wasn't going to tackle, and his attempts were more akin to an Italian goalkeeper diving for the cameras!

As with most clubs Frampton held an intra club trial game which is a full contact game with members of the first, second and third team sides mixed up by the coaches in such a way that the sides are equal but where they can also get to look at different pairings and combinations. Frampton's was to be in two Saturdays time with a Summer BBQ afterwards; it sounded like the perfect way to start the season and would give me some more time to meet some more faces and be involved in some team bonding (also known as get drunk)!

The Saturday soon came around after a couple more weeks of training, again with the intensity stepping up, it was a great day for a BBQ and a few drinks, although I'm not sure about Rugby as it was one of those rare summers where we had little rain and the pitch was more suitable for Cricket. However the Rugby would go ahead and the first two sides to start each other were announced. I was to play centre alongside Mark "tourettes" Chaplin or Chaps for short (not all nicknames were that witty). Chaps had the ability to split a word in half just to be able to get a swear word in, for example, 'absofuckinglutely'. On a Rugby field however Chaps was known for his tackling and would stop men twice his size in their tracks. Again I was happy to be next to him rather than opposite.

The game went by without incident and I remember scoring a couple of tries after taking a couple of defenders on the outside, and also making very few tackles thanks to my centre partner who seemed to want to hit everything. However I do remember tackling a man by the name of John Dean, who was one of the heftier backs, and although I stopped him I was definitely left knowing that he had run in to me!

John Dean was a no nonsense bloke who liked a beer, a good Rugby tour and at the time was living with Cornish. As I was new to the club and didn't really know many of the members that well I was more than vulnerable to odd wind up. I was like the apprentice you send to the shops to ask for a "long wait". After the game I was chatting to Tony Williams (Shag) and Paul Beet (Shag) who both took it upon themselves to inform me that John Dean and Cornish were in fact a couple, and that this is why they lived together. Now to look at John and Cornish this is not an assumption that any sane person would come to but nonetheless -who was I to argue, and why couldn't they be. I just assumed Shag and Shag were giving me more of an insight into each of the players. I couldn't be more wrong.

This wind up carried on right from the trial match in the summer all up until Christmas Eve where I was informed of my stupidity by complete chance. I was at my Grandparents for breakfast on Christmas Eve (as is tradition) and Dad, who was "working", stopped in for some food with his work colleague, Nigel. Now Nigel was also a regular at the Rugby club and new some of the lad's well from drinking round the village and also the local cricket team, so when I was recoiled the story that was told to me that summer's day and what had also been built up over the previous months, I was looked at with a look that said it all. "Stupid boy Pike". I had been well and truly had. Looking back it was beyond belief!

The first league game of the season was fast approaching and I was still unsure which of the three teams I would be selected for. In theory selection was always held on a Tuesday night after training by the three captains and the First XV manager.

However this should probably be called a first draft as come Saturday afternoon you can guarantee that it's not the same side that was selected on Tuesday usually due to work and sickness. One time someone was unavailable as the player in question was burying a horse! And yes he was in the front row!

Selection was probably another inaccurate description of what happens on the Tuesday night. In theory it would be a long debate about the form of individual players, potential prospects and giving players an opportunity. In practice the first team captain will have selected a team and the second and third team captain will fight it out between them with whoever is left. The form of players will be taken into account, however so will the personality as there are some players that will only play in certain teams and of course you have to account for illnesses such as Southmeaditus, Imonlyplayingathomeitus and the recurring itstoobloodywetandcolditus.

Selection was up on the board the following Thursday and I had been selected for the first team. I was pleased that I had impressed and made the first team straight away but I was still unsure if I was ready for senior Rugby. Saturday soon came around and the game passed without incident, or at least it must have as I can't remember whom we played or what the score was but I had survived and I must have done OK as I was picked for the following week.

The first game I can remember of any note was a home league fixture against Old Cryptians. It was a hot dry day and the ground being hard was perfect for running Rugby, which back when I was 18 was the type of Rugby I wanted to play - times have changed, or at least my role in the running style of Rugby has!

The day was memorable in that we ran out comfortable winners as wins had been few and far between at the start of the season but also I managed to score my first league try, and like buses I scored my second in the same game. One was put on a plate for me by my fellow no nonsense centre Chaps, whereas the other I managed to show my opposite number a clean pair of heels as I beat him for pace on the outside. Your first try for the club also means you have to get a jug in for the boys, which I was more than happy to do as my old man as always had come to watch, so therefore it was his wallet that was emptied.

The win made even better later on that week when I had a call from my Granddad telling me there were two photos of me in the local paper - one looked great as I was touching the ball down over the line, the second however looked as if Captain Birdseye, or someone who shares the same birth date had managed to tackle me as I was making a break.

The season continued to progress and the way things were going we were destined for mid table mediocrity. The season did then take a change of direction, especially for me. We were playing away at Aretians, a side with which I thought I might have joined and where a few schoolmates were playing. Aretians were top of the table and beating sides week in week out, so when our experienced Fly Half Weaves pulled his hamstring five minutes into the game things were not going our way.

Unfortunately there was no natural Fly Half replacement, so Zaff (who I'm not sure is the most qualified of backs experts) approached me and asked: "Can you kick?" To which I said yes I would have a go and he replied "right, then you are playing Fly Half today". Now I could kick, to a degree, and I was happy to kick but that didn't mean I could play Fly Half as the rest of the match and the following few matches proved.

As someone that had never played Fly Half and had only played a handful of senior matches I was thrown right in the deep end, and to start with I definitely sank! The following match we were away at Tewkesbury, a tough Gloucester team who didn't have much time for small village sides from Bristol. Again I was selected at ten and had been practicing kicking all week and was beginning to find some confidence. Ten minutes into the game we were three tries down and their 17stone beast of a Fly Half who looked like an old fashion Army Major had steam rolled me twice... just my bloody luck! Confidence gone! Their Fly Half scored five tries in that game and I can safely say I was at fault for at least four of them, possibly five. I probably should have received some cover from my open side but it was still shocking. It was a game I would not forget and from which I would still be feeling the aches and pains on Monday.

The game had obviously not gone well and I was feeling a little sorry for myself however everything on the pitch was soon forgotten when we were all having a few beers as we made our way back to Frampton with a few stop offs on the way. It was on these stop offs that talk began to move to this year's tour. This was something that I had never before experienced in any type of capacity. I had never been on any kind of sports' tour but I was very keen and had my name down as soon as it was mentioned. Listening to stories of past tours was thoroughly entertaining and I couldn't wait to have a weekend away. Some of this may also be down to the fact that I had also never been on a lad's holiday to Magaluf or Malia for example and I was keen to get involved.

The most difficult of a Rugby tour for some players isn't the excessive drinking or the public humiliation of being naked it's the moment you have to tell your wife or girlfriend that you are going. Back then I was one of those players, but I was determined I was going and that was that. Of course I had to make promises that were never going to be kept but my pass had been stamped. And the beauty of tour is of course, "what goes on tour stays on tour". So on the off chance I did end up in a strip club, no one would ever know. Things have changed dramatically as having a Welsh wife who grew up at the "House of Pain" means I have been organising the tour and she makes sure I'm on it!

It was also decided on the way home that we should have a proper "away" trip, and as luck would have it the first team captain Paul's 30th birthday was coming up which coincided with an away match against Painswick. It had the recipe to be a messy one.

Players and fans set off up to Gloucester in high hopes of picking up a win on the road, and there was to be no talk of the after match antics before the game - first and foremost we had a job to do. Painswick was a typical Gloucester side in that it was in the back ass end of nowhere with no civilisation for miles around, and many of the locals had the same surname. However, come Saturday at 14.30 they managed to field a side that was good enough to compete with any other in the league.

On this particular Saturday they were more than good enough to compete with us and tore us to shreds. I remember they had a full back that was also playing professional cricket for Gloucester and as a result was only allowed to play a certain level of Rugby. Unfortunately for us his level of Rugby was far superior to Gloucester One and any loose kick was punished.

At the end of the match the mood in the changing rooms was not good as we had just had our asses handed to us on a plate, however unlike other sports the mood was not going to stay for long. We had a 30th birthday to celebrate, and even more importantly it was our captain's. Whilst we were all getting geared up in our number ones, black trousers, blue shirt with the club badge and a green tie, Paul was being given an alternative choice of attire brought along by Shag.

Now as mentioned earlier Paul is an ex Para Trooper who is around 6ft tall, 16.5stone and built like a brick shithouse, so when he appeared in PVC shorts, waistcoat, boots and a flat cap it was a sight to behold and something that has continued to haunt me ever since. He looked like a cross between a Hell's Angel and a member of the Village People.

After a few beers in the Rugby club it was back on the bus with Dursley as the decided destination. Dursley was not what you would call a metropolis of nightlife but it had enough pubs and bars to keep us all entertained and to have a good night. As this was my first experience of being out properly with the Rugby club I was taken under the wing of the Slate twins. The night was moving along nicely and myself and the twins had found ourselves chatting to some of the local lovelies in a bar, and seemed to be doing very well. This may have been down to the fact that people from outside Dursley never visit and we were new faces rather than us being any good with the women, but I was happy to take either reason and we all looked set for a good night.

As the night wore on and more beer was consumed the inevitable seal was broken and therefore the gents was frequented after what seemed to be every sip of beer. During the seventh visit I was told by one of the more senior members of the club as he rather hurriedly exited the toilets that it was wheels on the bus and we were leaving this very moment. As a younger member of the team my place was not to question so I returned to the twins, told them the news and we were soon off, leaving the lovely locals to carry on their evening without us… what could have been?

Being none the wiser, small groups of the Fram party made their way back to the coach stopping off for the required healthy post match meal of kebab and chips not knowing what was about to unfold.

The Slate twins and myself took our seats on the middle of the coach, a minute or so later our PVC clad captain stumbled aboard and began to quickly swap various items of clothing with other members of the coach, mainly with Shag who was considerably smaller in size, which was not surprising given that one was a hooker and the other a winger. Again I was still none the wiser of the relevance of all the commotion.

Things became clearer however when a senior member of the coach stood up and informed us we were to say nothing if asked and to remain silent. This was then followed by two or three Police Officers boarding the coach looking for a large member of the Village People who had been involved in an altercation with the village idiot moments earlier.

When the Officers boarded the coach you could tell straight away that they realised they were fighting a losing battle. Dealing with 30 plus drunk Rugby blokes is not how they wanted to end their Saturday night shift in the sleepy town of Dursley, but nonetheless they asked our semi naked winger (he hadn't quite finished changing) to stand in front of the CCTV cameras, and again unsurprisingly it was confirmed that he was not the member that had been caught on CCTV having the altercation.

After some stern words from the officers to the boys, they thanked us for "sorting" the village idiot who had been in the altercation. He was now unconscious and we were kindly let on our merry way. Even kinder we were given a Police escort. Again this was another lesson in 'don't upset Captain Paul, especially on his birthday'.

The season wasn't going to plan in terms of results but in terms of me actually enjoying myself I was loving it. Though unfortunately me enjoying myself wasn't going to keep us from being relegated. What we needed was some experience at Fly Half, or at least someone that had played more than half a season of senior Rugby!

Luckily for Frampton, experience was something the club had in abundance, and if you had seen the average age of the playing members back then you would have agreed. The Messiah for the season was a player named Malcolm Soper.

Malcolm had been around the club for years though it was his Mother that I had gotten to know over the course of the first year. Sue was our ever-present lineswoman or referees assistant whatever the correct term is. My first introduction to Sue was one that I am not proud of and I blame my Football background. I was covering across in defence and made a poor attempt to tackle the opposition winger as he was flying down the wing. I thought I did enough to push him in to touch however Sue's flag stayed down and he scored a try.

Underneath the posts I did the Footballer thing. I moaned and whinged, claiming that his foot was on the line, and that Sue was cheating and didn't know what she was doing. At this point I was firmly put in my place: "shut the fuck up, Sue has been doing this for years, and is our linesman!" At this point I realised I had indeed been a prize dick. One, for not realising Sue was affiliated to the club (her flag was the club colours), and two for moaning in the first place. I apologised in the club after the game and thankfully all was forgiven otherwise it could have been a very short Rugby stint at the Fram.

The end of the season was looming and relegation was still a very real prospect. However with Malcolm now at the pivotal role of Fly Half we started to win and win ugly. Malcolm was dictating the games and we started to play more to our strengths, which at the time was our driving maul and close play as we had a very thick set of forwards - or is that a set of thick forwards? Either way, it was working, and by the skin of our teeth we avoided relegation.

Do the Shake and Vac

It was my first tour and I was excited and nervous; excited about a weekend with the boys and nervous about what I might have to do. It was 9.45 and I arrived at Crossbow in my 70s outfit, itinerary in hand and ready for a beer. Meet time was 10.00 but there was no danger of me being late - if there was an opportunity not to be punished I was going to take it!

There were a number of tour virgins on their way to Bournemouth whom I would share the pain with; Rocco, Gurn, Gary Plant, Big Craig, Son of Nige, and although he didn't know it yet Gary Paddock.

After a couple of pints in the clubhouse we all boarded the coach and set off for Bournemouth with a little detour en route. First stop was going be a country pub for some grub, the first slave auction and a few more beers, or so I thought. After 3 miles we stopped just outside Yate and 4 of the tour party jumped off the coach and ran into a house. I had no idea what was going on. Five minutes later they were back on the coach with Gary Paddock being carried on under their arms, he was flung onto a seat and we were off. Tour Kidnap, mission accomplished. Next stop, Country Pub.

Back on the coach the tour quickly began to gather pace as cans were being passed around the coach and it really did have a sense of the boys being allowed out to play for the only time all year and we going to make the most of it.

Unfortunately this was not the most modern of coaches, and probably didn't have all the amenities that were required for a group of men that had been constantly drinking since 10am. In fact the lack of a toilet I feared would be a big problem, especially as when I break the seal I tend to have the bladder the size of a pea! Luckily however there were experienced tourers aboard the fun bus and they had the forethought to combat the problem with a solution, albeit not the most hi tech solution and the thought process was probably very minimal - but we did have a bucket! One of the slaves was put in charge of it and had to hold it steady if anyone needed a pee. Thankfully it wasn't me! In more recent tours we have slowly progressed the bucket to a water dispenser turned upside down, which gave less chance of spillage and to then finally, a coach with a toilet! Genius!

We arrived at the country pub in good spirits and all informed the kitty master of our order. I was sticking to pints of lager (drink what I know and don't deviate; this was a marathon not a sprint). As we gathered, trays of sausage and chips were served and we all tucked into food that was purely functional - something to soak up the alcohol.

On the way to the pub the slaves/virgins, were apprehensive as we had heard that this was where the first slave auction would take place. On a standard Friday to Sunday tour the virgin members of tour would be split in two, with half of them being a slave on the Friday, the other half on the Saturday and then they would all be club slaves on the Sunday. This was only a one-night tour so slaves were split down the middle for the Saturday and Sunday. Being a slave would mean you would be sold to a consortium of tourers and you would be theirs to do with as they wished (although slave abuse was punishable in Kangaroo court). Thus continued from auction until midnight of the day in which they were purchased. Once you had completed your stint of being sold it did not then give you any rights on this tour as they would not come until your second tour. You still did as you were told.

The master of most ceremonies, Mike Weaver, stood up at the front of the Pub and started proceedings. First naming the slaves that would be auctioned off there and then, and I was one of them! Still I suppose it was better to get it out the way than to wait. Other members of the tour began to congregate into their consortiums and discuss who they were looking to buy and at what price. I had a feeling as the only member of the first team that was up for auction that I could be in a bit of trouble.

The first slave called up was Son of Nige (Ben to his friends), and I was wondering how this auction would take place, surely being in a pub it couldn't be too humiliating…wrong!
Son of Nige was made to stand on a chair so all the pub could see him and then remove his clothes so he could be "inspected". The inspection involved checking his teeth to see if they were all his own, his arse to see how firm it was usually with a gentle slap, general cleanliness and then the obvious - a lift, flick and even a sniff….

The bidding started, each bid increasing by ten pounds; some bids were purely to drive the price up, others, as they genuinely wanted the particular slave. As the bidding for Son of Nige drew to a close the bids became more unique and in the end he was sold for £62.55p.

I was next up, clothes off I climbed up onto the chair. The inspection started, I had all my own teeth, a good arse (if I do say so myself), and was genuinely well groomed and clean. Then came the bit I was dreading.

Now I had a nickname that my friends called me. This was not a well-known nickname as I had kept it well and truly under wraps. It wasn't something I wanted to be made public. The nickname was Gonzo. It all came about when playing golf (another story) and trying to put off my two mates Andy and Dan. I stood behind them with the old boy poking through my shorts. Andy's response word for word was "impressive but why does it bend like that, it's like Gonzo's nose". The nickname stuck.

Mike Weaver was also known at the club as a bit of a cock connoisseur; if you mentioned a playing member to Mike I'm pretty sure he could tell you if there was anything out of the ordinary to do with their member. Anyway the final part of the inspection began, and sure enough comments like "you wouldn't want it behind your ear for a pencil", "it has a significant kink", "it can look round corners" were made. In fact the bend in the old boy is still continually mentioned, once at an annual dinner, and the direction of the bend was even asked in a Rugby club quiz night!

The bidding started and again each bid increased by ten pounds a time, finally "sold for £85". I was looking around the pub to see who was successful in their bidding, and there it was the sight I or no other slave wanted to see…. The consortium consisting of Badger, Shag (Tony Williams), Captain Paul Beet, Dave "Uncle Albert" Crew, and Malcolm Soper were there with a glint in their eyes and their arms up!

Badger, Shag and Paul were all fair in what they would dish out and I knew I would be looked after but they were all deviants and I knew I would definitely not be given an easy ride. This was going to be interesting.

I walked over to my masters looking at who I had just been bought by, first mistake. I was informed I was no longer allowed to look at them in the eye. Next I was told that they no longer wanted to be referred to by their real names but now as Master Barry, Master Steve, Master Reginald, Master Tom and Master Lucas and if or when I got it wrong I would be punished. Brilliant!

As a standard rule all slaves would make the trips to the bar to buy the drinks from money given to them by their masters. After the first round a good slave would not need to ask what was wanted or when they should go, they should monitor their masters pint glasses and make sure a pint is waiting for them as they finished. As a treat I was told by my masters I could drink what I wanted, which was a result as at the time I only really drank lager. Unfortunately Master Lucas (Captain Paul) had other ideas and with every pint of lager I also had to order myself a Pernod and Black with a glacier cherry. Yummy!

As with all tours it's nice to think of something original for your slave to do and if possible to also amuse everyone else in the bar or wherever you may be at the time. For me this was definitely the case. Every time the word "telephone" was said I had to perform the shake n vac advert with singing and the actions reminiscent of the advert from the 80s, no matter where I was. I can still remember the words now:

Do the Shake 'n Vac, and put the freshness back
Do the Shake 'n Vac and put the freshness back
When your carpet smells fresh, your room does too
Every time you vacuum, remember what to do
Do the Shake 'n Vac and put the freshness back.

After a few more pints we were back on the coach all well lubricated and en route to our next stop, Dorchester, here we would be playing the first tour match. By the end of the coach trip I was without a doubt, struggling. I was however determined to keep going and prove that I would be a good slave.

Again with a match approaching it was time to focus and be serious; this was easier said than done! The side was announced and I was in my favoured position of centre, I got kitted up and went outside to warm up. This unfortunately is all I remember of the game as the next thing I knew I was being woken up with the Cock Connoisseurs appendage being dabbled on to my nose as I lay sound asleep or passed out depending on how you viewed it, on the physio bench.

I am told that after the warm up, I came back in to the changing room and passed out on the physio bench, it was decided that it would probably be best if I were left there! Unfortunately Fram also lost the game but in good touring spirit Master Lucas let them know we weren't going to be pushovers and chinned his opposite number. Perhaps falling asleep wasn't a bad idea!

After a shower, to wake me up more than anything, we headed in to the clubhouse for a few more pints, and for me to continue my ongoing performances of the Shake n' Vac routine. At this rate it wouldn't be long before an Oscar was mine.

It is tradition on any Fram Rugby tour that all virgin tourers as well as being auctioned off have to take part in the customary naked run and if the location allows, or sometimes if it doesn't - a naked swim. It was time for the run and it was also decided that the run would be handicapped so all front row forwards would be set off first, followed by second row, back row and so on. Unfortunately for me this meant I would be one of the last to be released, even more unfortunately for me my masters warned me that if I didn't win there would be consequences. I tried to reason with them but as a slave I had no rights so it was pointless. Plus as I had napped during the game and let my masters down I needed to win for redemption and to restore some pride.

We were set off one by one, first Big Craig then son of Nige, followed by Garry Paddock, Gurn, Rocco and finally me. We had to run the length of the pitch, through the posts and back to the clubhouse. It was more than my life was worth not to win that race so off I went in pursuit of the naked hairy men in front of me (I never thought I would write those words)! Luckily for me I had a bit of pace about me, and compared to the others I was fresh, one by one I passed them until eventually I was leading, I was not going to let this lead slip and soon crossed the line in first place. I was hoping this would go someway in making my masters happy.

As all the slaves congregated back in the clubhouse doorway hoping to be allowed to put our clothes back on there was a shout from Master Tom (Badger) "make them wrestle on the bouncy castle". We were all a little perplexed.We had no idea where he thought we would be able to find a bouncy castle at a Rugby club! Master Tom however had done some investigating, and had noticed there was a bouncy castle set up around the corner of the clubhouse ready for the Children at a wedding reception that were due to arrive later on that day. Badger led us like the pied piper to the castle where he ordered us in one by one to begin our Battle Royal. It was a pile of hairy, sweaty, flabby nakedness. Not a pretty sight. Even less of a pretty sight was having big Craig (around 6ft and 17stone) flop on you in his naked state. I still wake up at night crying.

Badger, or Gary Caldicot as it says on his Birth Certificate, was a senior member of the club and a scrum half by trade. He was the type of scrum half that Fram forwards loved and that every member of the opposition hated. He was also a firm believer in 'if it s lying in front of the ball, stamp on it, no messing about'. This did tend to get Badger in a bit of trouble either with referees or opposition forwards. As much of an irritant as he was on the field he had the ability to be as equally as irritating off it, and if there was a chance to cause some kind of mischief you could be sure that he might have something to do with it.

Eventually we were all allowed to return to a state of dress and rejoin the tour party in the clubhouse. Apparently our clubs naked antics had not gone down to well with some members of the wedding party who had arrived earlier than expected. Not wanting to out stay our welcome we retuned to the coach excited about hitting the Bournemouth nightlife.

We arrived at our Bournemouth Premier Inn blurry eyed and dragging tails but we were still keen as mustard. As with any good Rugby tour, rooms are allocated randomly with no bias whatsoever.... I had been allocated a double room with Spud (Martin Hill). I hadn't gotten to know Spud much over my first season but I did know that as a virgin tourer he was a perfect room mate as he wouldn't be interested in stitching me up and he wasn't a deviant. Result!

The plan was, check in, the three well knows S's and then out again. We met in the lobby and we were off out, all slaves were to stay with their masters until midnight or told otherwise. So off I went in to the Bournemouth night at the mercy of the great consortium. After having a few beers in a Wetherspoons (luckily the Pernod had stopped) we moved on to our next watering hole where we queued outside.

The venue was trendy and everyone entering was smartly

dressed. We were now out of our 70s costumes and were dressed to impress. Soon we were at the front of the queue having waited around 10 minutes. Now I'm not sure if it was that obvious that it may not have been a bar we usually frequent but as soon as got to the front the bouncer said to us "you do know this is a gay bar?" Obviously we didn't but Captain Paul, Shag, Badger and Dave Crew were thirsty and it didn't matter one jot so in we went. Malcolm however wasn't so keen and shuffled in and then went very very quiet for the next hour or so, only ever muttering "can we leave yet?"

One thing that the masters may use their slaves for is going over to break the ice with groups of girls, and sure enough after I had again been to the bar for everyone I was pointed in the direction of a small group of lovelies and told to go and see if I could bring them back. To many tour slaves this may have been their worst nightmare, however I was not a shy retiring 18 year old, I was an 18 year old who was more than willing and happy to chat to as many girls as I could point a stick at (excuse the pun). I also wasn't that worried about being rejected; my general rule was "if you throw enough shit, some will eventually stick".

Being a slave on tour and being ruled by five men gives you an easy opening line with the ladies and allows you to play the timid sympathy card, a card I was more than happy to use. After a quick introduction and explaining that we weren't from the area and asking if they would mind coming over and giving us some ideas of where to go they soon tottered over to the masters. Having girls to talk to in a gay bar also made Malcolm more at ease.

The girls spoke to us for a while telling us lots of different bars to go to and clubs we could end up in; there were Vodka bars, your generic Australian bar, different Wetherspoons - we certainly had lots of options. As soon as they left us to our own devices we ignored all suggestions, engaged our inner Neanderthal and headed straight to the nearest strip club, via Burger King. Burger and Boobs.

The end of the night really is where you are looked after on a tour; providing you have performed you slave duties. I was being taken to my first ever strip club, For Your Eyes Only. My entry was paid for, my beer was paid for (as it had been all night) and as it was now past midnight there was nothing left for me to do. I could even leave if I wanted, though I was going nowhere... there were naked girls! I was then rewarded for my day's work by being allowed to choose any dancer I wanted for a private dance. It was almost like being told I had passed my initiation and I was now accepted.

The rest of the night passed without incident and it was time to return to the Premier Inn and get into bed with Spud. After ending the night at a strip club this was definitely a dramatic change of scenery, and a sure way to calm any previous excitement.

Sunday morning came and everyone was feeling a little worse for wear, however the best thing for any hangover was hair of the dog. That said I think hair of the dog is meant to be a pint to take the edge off, not another 10 pints to put the edge back on. So it was bacon, sausage, egg beans and that well-known breakfast drink, lager.

On Rugby tour, as well as the main rule of "what goes on tour, stays on tour" there were also a number of other rules that must be obeyed, one of which is "no phones'. This Sunday however was Mother's Day, and it was agreed that everyone should make a call to their Mum and tell them they loved them… Rugby players do have a softer side.

We were all aboard the coach ready to leave Bournemouth and next on the itinerary was meant to be a naked swim. As we pulled away from the hotel I thought this might have been a bullet that I had dodged. As we drove along a dual carriageway there was a shout of "stop the coach" when out of the window to the left was the sea. Bollocks.

All slaves were ordered off the coach on to the side of the dual carriageway and told to strip naked - there seemed to be a theme about this tour. There was no race this time, we were just told we had to enter the water and ensure our head was under the water at some point. With passing cars beeping their horns and waving at us we entered the water and as expected it was freezing and cold water does nothing for your ego when you are naked!
Another tour tradition was completed and all the slaves were pretty happy, until we realised we had just swam alongside a sewer pipe! A hangover the next day may be the least of our worries.

Back on the coach we set off for Salisbury where we were to play a 6 a side Rugby tournament on half pitches. We had links with Salisbury through Richard Lloyd, an ex Fram scrum half, so it was an obvious place to stop. Tour games on a Sunday are never easy as there were a lot of heavy heads, and for the majority playing two games in two days was a challenge. In fact for some getting out of bed on a Sunday after Saturday's match was an achievement.

Arriving at Salisbury we soon realised we were two short from the original tour party. This just goes to show that the tour itinerary was there for a reason, and if you missed the time that was on the bit of paper the tour will go on without you.

The two guilty members of the tour party arrived at Salisbury in a taxi an hour or so later, £85 lighter and in the same clothes they had on the night before. It was an expensive walk of shame, but on the plus side from their point of view they were too late to play in the tournament and could watch with a pint in hand. Something to remember for the future maybe?

Sunday was an enjoyable day with the tournament played in good spirits, and to top it off it was won by a team entered by the mighty Fram. Hospitality was enjoyed in the clubhouse before we were on our way back to Crossbow. It was a great first tour and there was no way it was going to be my last. More than anything I wanted to have the chance to buy a tour virgin!

When the coach pulled into the car park back at Crossbow there were a number of tourers that were not yet ready to call it a day and were eager to make tour last as long as possible. As a result a table at the local curry house was booked. We arrived at the curry house in good spirits and were all still very much in the tour mode. Those that had gone out on the Sunday night hoping for a quiet meal were soon to be very disappointed.

The curries and beer were ordered and we were soon tucking into probably the most nutritious meal we had eaten all weekend. With it being tour, and as Tony Williams (Shag) was there, mischief was imminent - and mischief for Shag means getting naked. Soon there were twenty of us sat in the local curry house on a Sunday night all naked. The owners of the curry house weren't overly impressed with their latest diners, but a table of twenty drunken Rugby players is not the easiest group of people to argue with. However we were bribed with a few free bottles of red and we soon all had our clothes back on.

At the end of every season there is the annual dinner. Always a great event organised by the wonderful WAGS of Frampton Rugby Club. This is an event enjoyed by all. Unfortunately this was not the case in my first year as there were still a few members of the tour party that were suffering the after effects of swimming next to a sewer pipe. I'm sure this was slave abuse!

Now F**k off back to Bristol

I had finished my final year at sixth form and had obtained the required UCAS points to decide which University I was going to attend, and it was a similar decision to the one I faced a year earlier with regards to which Rugby club I was going to study at - although not quite as important.

I could go to Bristol University, but after visiting the open day this was very similar to choosing to play for Clifton.

I could decide on Cardiff University, but at the end of the day this is in Wales and I'm not sure if they played Rugby there (please keep reading Mr(s) Jones, Jenkins, Davies, Evans, Williams). There is a twist later.

Or I could go to Bristol Universities more modern, down to earth Brother, the University West of England, or UWE, as it is better known. My decision was also made easier as it was where my two muckers, Andy and Dan were going. Andy had similar ideas on what he wanted to do in terms of career, and Dan just copied Andy's UCAS application. Oh and my girlfriend at the time was also going there.

During the first week of University there is, of course, the freshers fare. Lots of stalls with all the different clubs and societies trying to get you to join up. I was keen to join the Rugby club so walked over and grabbed the information about where and when the training and trials were. I was quite excited to be playing Rugby against my age group, with a new set of lads and having that first season experience again.

Training was on a Monday night; it was a strange affair and nothing like what I was used to at the Fram. We were split into forwards and backs and went off to run some handling drills followed by some backs moves - I recognised the moves, they just had different names to Fram. At the end of the session we were asked if we could attend a trial match on the Saturday, and were told that the Freshers team generally played on a Saturday afternoon. That was the end of UWE Rugby for me; Saturday afternoon I played for Fram.

As it had only been one season where I hadn't been playing Football I still felt I could hold my own and more to the point I didn't want to miss out on the socialising aspect of Uni. As luck would have it my old centre back partner at Frampton was running the UWE Football 3rd team, so although I had missed the initial trials I was in, and therefore Wednesday evenings were sorted.

Pre-season at Frampton hadn't officially started but a number of lads used to carry on turning up on a Thursday night for a kick about with the round shaped ball. I think this was more of an excuse to not go to B&Q or decorate the house, however it was a run around for an hour and helped to keep everyone in some kind of shape.

The pre pre-season kickabout at Crossbow would have been an eye opener for anyone that decided to watch and would certainly not be mistaken for a "normal" game of Football. There were varying degrees of ability when it came to Football. Some thought they were Maradona, where in reality they were more like Madonna. There was the front row brigade who used to like standing up front trying and tending not to move much more than a 3-meter radius. There was the back five in the scrum, who tended to be more intent on kicking anything that moved and wasn't shaped like a ball. And of course there were us fancy backs, who all thought we could have played either sport: some could, most couldn't.

The start of the season also brought about the return of Keith Weaver after knee surgery. I had heard a lot about Keith during my first season at Frampton, usually in sentences like "We really miss Keith Weaver", "We might have won that today with Keith", and so needless to say he had quite a reputation at the club, and rightly so; his name was on the player of the year trophy more times than not.

Keith was affectionately known as Mr Tickle due to his incredibly long arms and his ability to get hold of anyone that got too close. As the start of the season began it soon became evident that Keith was exactly what we had been missing in the previous year. A number 7 that could read the game, steal countless balls, win his lineout ball and most importantly for me would tackle anything that moved.

The second season was very similar to the first, with exotic away trips up the M5 to Brockworth, Tewkesbury and Bream. The trip to Bream was one that was always dreaded, it lies in the heart of the Forest of Dean and from the size of the players they put out on a Saturday it was clear that the inhabitants slept in grow bags. They were all monsters.

This particularly Saturday we were struggling with numbers and a few old boys helped us out by coming out of retirement to wear the Fram jersey. One in particular was Sean Hodges, or Reggie. Reg was one of the most talented backs to ever play for Frampton, either at Fly Half or full back and in his youth even managed an England Colt's cap. However playing away to Bream no matter where you have played in the past, or whom you have played for in the past was a totally different kettle of fish.

We pulled in to the car park at Bream after driving through villages that wouldn't have been out of place in a J R Tolkien novel and congregated outside the clubhouse. The place seemed to be very empty considering we were meant to be playing in just over an hour. As we were wondering what was going on we were met by one of the club's officials, who for sake of argument we shall call Mr Baggins.

Mr Baggins looked very confused to see us as he explained that they were not expecting to have a match today and that we must have been mistaken, as there were no players currently in the clubhouse or changing rooms. After a number of phone calls to fixture secretaries and the league representative we were in the right place, and Bream were told they had to fill the fixture or forfeit the game. We all thought we would soon be back in our cars having collected the easiest away win of the season.

Any other club with an hour before kick off would struggle to find fifteen players, let alone fifteen players that could play first team Rugby, however Mr Baggins wandered off and made a few phone calls. Within ten minutes they had a team including replacements (mostly consisting of Orcs), and the game was on. We were still confident of picking up a win; I mean this couldn't be a strong team having been put together at the last minute.

Ten minutes in to the match and it soon became very clear that we had been stitched up in the car park. This was by no means a team that had been put together at the last minute. They were beating us up upfront, running us ragged out wide and making poor Reg run from side to side at full back. He was definitely not rolling back the years. The pattern of the match continued throughout and the full time whistle could not come soon enough. When the full time whistle finally did arrive we had been comprehensively beaten. The usual tunnels formed with the obligatory three cheers, and then there was a lovely shout from the men from middle earth, "now f**k off back to Bristol!" I had the feeling they didn't like us city folk!

Frampton is a village and parish in South Gloucestershire, south west England on the River Frome. The village is 8 miles north-east of the city of Bristol.
The village has evolved from a once rural Gloucestershire village, to a partial dormitory village for Bristol. The population is around 6,800 and is increasing.

As with all Rugby clubs there are a number of non-playing members that ensure the smooth running of the Rugby club, whether that is the junior or the senior section or helping behind the bar on a Saturday. Within our club the WAGS were a huge proportion of the volunteers and deserved to be rewarded with a night that was solely for their benefit. If truth were told they probably deserve more than a night, but that's all they were getting. This season a ladies night had been organised, I think by the ladies themselves, which probably defeated the purpose, but it was the first one of its time at the club and promised to be a good night.

You may be wondering why I thought it would be a good night, as surely with a ladies night it should be for the ladies, and it was. It was to be a sit down meal, at the club, cooked by our resident chefs John Maidstone and Zaff (using mamas secret recipe), a few games hosted by the master of ceremonies for the evening, Malcolm Soper, and finally a stripper. One thing that the evening also needed however was a group of young, fit and willing Rugby players that were willing to serve the food wearing nothing but some tight shorts, a dickey bow and a smile to a hundred or so women. Now where would they find them?!

The night soon came around and there was myself, Shag, Cornish, Rocco, and a couple of other likely lads all kitted down ready for the evening to start. Rocco was a scrum half in his first season with the seniors having gone through the youth teams at Fram. To begin it was a quiet affair but as soon as the drinks started flowing, everything changed, and to make matters worse there had been a cancellation. No stripper.

While the ladies weren't aware of the unfortunate cancellation we began to serve them their food. Now I'm not saying being a waiter is an easy job as I have done my stint at a well known Pizza chain, but it is most definitely made a lot harder when there are wandering hands while you are carrying plates of hot food. This was only a taste of things to come.

Malcolm was now left with the unenviable task of having to fill time, which meant games. The games were not your usual dinner party games. One game involved just one from the group taking a drink of Baileys and then a number of the ladies deciphering whom it was by taking it in turns to kiss the line. This was great fun, though a little odd having to kiss a number of teammates WAGS. After the games the night turned out like many others - into carnage - and my over riding memory is running out into the car park with Rocco scared. Looking back I wish I didn't run away- if I could have my time again!

The following Saturday at Rugby as I pulled in to the car park Badger was there. I thought nothing of it, then suddenly it hit me, I had kissed Mrs Badger during the Baileys game! As I stepped out the car, Badger called me over, "Shit!" As I got to where Badger was standing he said to me, "it's a good job I like you and you were a good slave" - PHEW!

Back at university on a Wednesday afternoon I had just played my first match for the UWE 3rd team at Football, and already something was very noticeable. At no point was the referee a W*nker or did he get a decision wrong. "Yes sir", "sorry sir", "and my mistake sir". This was picked up on by the other lads in the team and I was soon the butt of a few jokes.

Being the first match of the season and with this being University there was the obvious need for some kind of initiation. We (the freshers) were all told to be at the Walkabout on Corn Street for 7pm. When we all arrived the air was filled with nerves, no one sure exactly what we would have to do, but I wasn't all that concerned considering I had survived my first Rugby tour this couldn't be that bad! I mean it was very unlikely I was going to have to sing the shake n vac or wake up with a cock being dabbled on my nose.

We were all called upstairs and put in to groups of around 8 people. In the room were a number of different stations around the outside with 4 bins in the middle. We were then told we had to visit each station, take the drink or food that was on offer and continue around the room as fast as we could. It didn't sound too bad, I mean we were students and it was free food and drink!

The stations were as follows:

1. *Pint of Bitter*
2. *A fun size Mars bar*

3. *Pint of Lager*
4. *A raw sprout*
5. *A shot of tequila*
6. *Tablespoon of mixed cocoa and chilli powder*
7. *Shot of hot dog brine*
8. *A pint of cider with the hot dog inside*

I was placed in group number 3 and it was soon our turn to tackle the initiation. We set off at a good pace with a couple of the lads really setting the standard. The first 3 stations were tackled with ease. The raw sprout however soon halted proceedings as these were not easy to chew, but were soon managed by all. At station number 5 we had our first casualty, there was now sick in the bin. The cocoa/chilli powder was another roadblock as again this was not easy to swallow and the group soon began to spread out. Now came one of the worst things I have ever tasted - the shot of brine - there was now a lot of sick in the bin! Thankfully none of it mine. The final station was a treat more than anything, I was just happy to get rid of the taste of the brine!

Of all the freshers there were only 3 of us that had managed a clear round with no sick penalties, and I can also proudly say we were all local lads from Bristol. I would like to take this opportunity to thank Badger, Shag and Captain Paul for unknowingly prepping me on my first tour.

The first part of the season before Christmas had been a mixed bag of results but we had improved on last season and we weren't going to be dragged in to the relegation dogfight as long as we could keep on improving and stay clear from the injuries that had plagued us the previous year.

All Rugby clubs form part of the local community; just how big a part depends on the geography, the success of the club, and most importantly how much the Rugby club is willing to give back. Fram is very much a community club. It's a club where all ages and abilities are welcome from minis to vets and 3 senior teams who take the field on a Saturday afternoon. As well as the Rugby side there are also social events for the community, including quiz nights, BBQ's and parties for Christmas and New Year.

It was coming up to Christmas and the idea had been banded about the club that we should produce a Calendar to raise some money. Now with us being a Rugby club there were 2 options: the pictures could be action shots taken from a Saturday afternoon, or as with most things that involved Rugby clubs they could be done naked.

The decision to make the calendar a naked calendar was quick and unanimous; it was as if someone had asked Zaff if he was having a pint after the game. A photographer was found and soon a date was set. All players that wanted to be in the calendar had to be at Crossbow an hour before training was meant to start.

On the day of the calendar shoot it was no surprise that there was an above average turnout for training. Some people will do anything for their five minutes of fame, and Rugby players will not miss an opportunity to take their clothes off. (The same however cannot be said for Football players. The UWE were also producing a naked calendar with each sport having being designated one month. We were March. Again those that wanted to be included in the calendar were given the time and destination. Of the 4 squads only 5 people turned up, I was one of them.

Rugby players and getting naked were two things that tend to go hand in hand. This could not be more truthful when it came to Tony Williams (Shag), if he could Shag would do everything naked. There have been numerous occasions when he and people around him find themselves naked: the curry after Bournemouth tour, a Chinese for his birthday, playing pool in the Rugby club and on one occasion at training.

We had arrived for training, slightly optimistically as there was snow on the frozen ground. Due to the conditions the turnout wasn't great and there was talk of calling training off and going back home. Though we had made the effort to get to Crossbow so we would at least go out and have a run around and play touch Rugby. Now as this was not a normal training session Shag wanted to change some of the rules, and who were we to argue. With this being Shag it was again inevitable that the rules would somehow involve getting naked, even with the snow. Sure enough this was the case, the rule was every time a try was scored, the opposition had to remove clothing. Within twenty minutes we were all naked (apart from socks and boots) playing Rugby in the snow!

The calendar was a good success and definitely made it easy to buy Christmas presents for the relatives, girlfriend, girlfriend's relatives and work colleagues: they were all getting a naked picture of my team and me.

One of the highlights of the social calendar at the Rugby club was Boxing Day. The morning consisted of the junior age groups playing against their parents with a few of the seniors thrown in to make up the numbers. The last game was the Colts playing as close to a first team as was available. This game was always hard work as the main things on the youngster's minds were smashing us. The games however were just an excuse to get to the club early, the real fun happened afterwards.

On Boxing Day morning I would meet Ginger Jonesy at the bottom of his road en route to Crossbow house. Jonesy is a couple of years younger than me though knew almost every drinking game that was played. The meet time would depend on whether we were intending on playing Rugby that morning. To start with it was like any other day at the Rugby club, general socialising with a few pints, but this soon changed when the long tables came out and were placed in the back room.

There would be the usual suspects sat around the tables. As well as Jonesy and I there would be Rocco, Shag, the Cobley clan (only one of them played Rugby, Rob, but it was a family day and all were welcome) and a number of others all keen and eager to play some drinking games.

Jonesy would be the games master with his extensive knowledge and ensure that all the standard drinking rules would apply; no pointing, left hand drinking, no swearing, no names etc. Shag was the designated snitch, just in case Jonesy missed anything. The first game would usually be something simple like 21's, though depending on how much you had to drink previously would depend on exactly how simple. Because of the morning matches you could guarantee there would usually be a few members of the Colts side that would be joining in the Boxing Day games for the first time. To Jonesy and Shag, these were considered fresh meat and it didn't usually take long before they were picked on. Unfortunately with drinking games, if you are bad you are only going to get worse with the more you drink.

On one such occasion the newbie to the table was Rocco's cousin, Hannah. As well as being Rocco's cousin, and very good-looking, she was also the daughter of ex Bristol and Bath utility back Barry Whitehead. This was priceless.

Barry was a senior member of the club and had been involved in pretty much everything within the club at some point. It is safe to say that Barry was Frampton through and through and over the years Barry had worked tirelessly for the club both on and off the field of play. At one point Barry was so involved in trying to improve the club there were rumours of a park and ride.

The games moved on from 21's to tap taps, Bo Derricks Tits, to Whiz Boing Bounce and then the crowd favourite - Cantonese Whiz Boing Bounce. The games mixed in with the standard drinking rules soon had everyone a little bit worse for wear. Hannah however was a lot worse for wear and soon decided enough was enough. For Shag this was mission accomplished. (Game rules can be found at the back of the book).

The rest of the season went as expected and we finished just mid table, never troubling for promotion or relegation. Keith Weaver was rightly awarded player of the season for his countless man of the match performances. Even when he had an off game the man was still immense.

There are Rugby players and there are those that play Rugby

As a team we were improving year on year and were becoming one of the stronger teams in the Gloucester One division. For the upcoming season there was a change in the coaching set up and Tony Slate (Dad of Liam and Tom) would be the forwards coach and Dave Ashwin (Dad of me) would coach the backs.

This was not the first time I had been coached by my Dad. First it was playing Football for the cubs, when apparently he would despair as I would stand in the cold sucking the sleeve of my shirt. Then he became the coach of the local Cricket team and coached from under 11s through 16s; however it was usually down to me to make sure we had a team by asking everyone in school that day. Finally he was coaching a sport he knew something about.

Early on in the season we faced our main rivals Chipping Sodbury. The past few seasons these games had not been profitable for us with Sodbury beating us and even being promoted. Chipping Sodbury was not necessarily the closest club in terms of distance, however the club was always on a par in terms of standard. We would drink on Chipping Sodbury high street and as a result a number of the players knew each other. There was always some added spice in this fixture and it didn't take much to get the players up for this one, more than anything bragging rights were at stake.

We started brightly with the forwards putting on the pressure and we were soon six points to the good thanks to the boot of Mike Weaver. Weaves was not able to make the breaks he used to back when he was younger but he was still deadeye with the boot and given that Mike was not as small as he used to be it was now like having an extra back row forward. He was a smart player and as a result used to find himself on the back of driving mauls when the forwards were close to scoring and sure enough he would pop up with the ball. It was a perfect example of Mike's mantra "there are Rugby players, and there are those that play Rugby".

The game ebbed and flowed with neither side pulling away. With the game so close and every decision potentially being crucial it soon began to boil over and was only a matter of time before there was a flash point. Sure enough there was a high tackle on Barry, and up it went. Now a high tackle on Barry was sometimes a little hard to avoid as Barry was slightly vertically challenged, and also had a minor case of short man syndrome.

After the dust had settled and Weaves had kicked the resulting penalty we were five points up with only minutes to play, however we were not done yet and there was still time for icing on the cake. After a great break from Shag the ball was quickly recycled and the ball found its way along the backline to Barry. After the earlier incident Barry was in one of those moods where the ball was going no further, however he was also in one of the moods where he was going to score. He stepped his man and then glided past the full back to secure the victory. Retribution had been served.

As well as starting the season with new coaches I had reached the sandwich year in my degree course and as a result was working full time for the first time in my life, at Churngold Construction. Churngold had strong links with an up and coming team in the Gloucester leagues, Old Colstonians, and it was not uncommon for their workers to wear the Old C's shirt on a Saturday afternoon. In fact on my first day in work I was asked if I played Rugby, who I played for, and then if I would like to join Old C's. I'm surprised I got the job not playing for them!

There was also a new first team captain at the helm. It was a big unit of a second row by the name of Mike Prosser. Mike was a no nonsense second row that at times could be wound up the wrong way, and when standing at 6ft 5 and 18 stone plus you don't really want to make him angry. Mike also had a more philosophical side and loved a question; especially it seemed during training when you were stood around in the freezing cold and pouring rain. Mike just liked to be sure of things.

The season had been going well and we found ourselves in the top half of the table for the first time since I had arrived and there was talk of really pushing for promotion. The next Saturday came and we were on our travels to play against Old Bristolian's. Old B's, like Old C's was a team founded by a group of old School chums after they had to leave their school on which Hogwarts was based.

This particularly Saturday we were on the wrong end of a few bad refereeing decisions, which ultimately proved costly as we fell to a narrow defeat. Now as mentioned Mike could have a short fuse and something this Saturday had manage to trigger that fuse quite spectacularly. Rather than wait for the usual tunnel at the end of the game and the customary three cheers Mike made his way to the changing rooms, and as Mike was a man of sizeable proportions it was decided it was best not to stand in his way and let him carry on.

When we finally did arrive back at the changing rooms it was noted that the room was suddenly not as private as it once was.

Mike in his anger had decided to punch the door. Now if I had decided to take this action I would be on my way to A&E with a broken hand and the door would not have even splintered, however with Mike punching the door there was now a gaping hole and Mike was still in no mood to question or reason with.

It was decided the best course of action to take, instead of confessing to Old B's, was to place a piece of paper over the Mike fist shaped hole. Like in many changing rooms around the land there were pieces of paper put up on the wall giving tour dates, match fines, motivational words, that kind of information so this was easily and successfully achieved. Problem averted.

During the season Rugby was becoming more and more popular across the nation as England were embarking on their 2003 World cup campaign and were progressing comfortably through the rounds including a comprehensive victory over the Welsh (Sorry couldn't resist). As the final against Australia was approaching everyone was excited about watching the game and hopefully getting into the party spirit and finally revelling in some sporting glory. Obviously this excitement was rife at the Rugby club with everyone being keen spectators, however there was an issue. The RFU in their infinite wisdom had still scheduled match fixtures for local sides for the Saturday of the World Cup Final. Plans for a Leo Sayer had to be put on hold, as after watching England in the World Cup Final we had no choice but to prepare for a league fixture, again up the M5 to Gloucester to play Brockworth!

Saturday arrived and everyone gathered at the Rugby club for breakfast and to ensure they had a good seat for the match. The atmosphere was building nicely and as we all had to stay off the ale a walk round the village was planned for later that evening to hopefully celebrate. It was odd to see those that you usually enjoy a few pints with after a game drinking orange juice during the most important Rugby match of our lifetime, however we had a job to do later and everyone was committed.

The game as I'm sure you are all aware was tense, nail biting but the result was never in doubt (much), and England was the World champion.

After the game we all set off the M5 and soon arrived at Brockworth, after the usual routine of everyone getting kitted out and strapped up we went outside for the warm up. Usually our warm up was a gentle affair with a small game of touch, some stretching and finally hitting the tackle bags. Today however was different, the coach (Dad), had decided the warm up was going to be a bit more intense and we were soon getting a sweat on.

The reason for this soon became clear as one person in particular was struggling, prop Mark Smith. Now Smither wasn't the fittest man on the team and I'm sure he doesn't list running as one of his past times; the fact he was a prop confirms this. However I had never seen anyone throw up during the warm up of a game, pre season yes, but not before a game. The reason for Smither throwing up wasn't to do with his fitness level but more to do with the 6 pints he had in the morning watching the final. I hadn't noticed he was drinking, however the old man had been in the police for thirty years and not much gets past him, especially when its from a member of the front row.

The game was a non-event, we ran out comfortable winners beating Brockworth though to be honest this was not the Rugby story for today and we were all much more interested in getting back to Frampton to have a good beer and revel in England's victory.

We returned to Crossbow and when we walked in it was like the party had not stopped from the morning. The plan was to have a few beers in the Rugby club then have a wander round the village stopping in each pub for a few before ending up at the Rugby club's favourite pub, the Rising Sun. This was pretty much always the plan on a Rugby night out when we were staying local; there might be a slight deviation where the final destination was the Frampton Balti, and the club's curry connoisseur Cornish usually instigated this. Such was David of Cornwall's knowledge I used to actually doubt the origin of the curry.

In the league our form had dipped and we were back in mid table mediocrity, but we had put together a cup run and found ourselves in the final of the Charles Saunders Combination cup. Any cup final whatever level you are playing at is a big deal, and this was no exception.

Our opponents in the cup final were Old Colstonians. Old C's were in the division below us but were sitting pretty at the top of their league and had been beating teams comfortably all year by playing running Rugby. With our opponents being Old C's it also spiced up the banter in work, where I was massively outnumbered.

The final was to be played on a Friday night under lights at Clifton Rugby Club where I had played my Colt Rugby. Old Colstonians and Clifton were not too dissimilar in their pedigree in that the majority of their team had a double-barrelled surname, wore tweed and had never even heard of Primark.

The training session on the Thursday before the final was just a light run out, running through our patterns of play and talking about how we were going to attack the game. You could tell by the attitude at training that night the players were up for this.

The day of the final came and I had to go to work. I remember being in work and they decided today was the day they were going to have an office reshuffle and move all the desks and cupboards around. I refused, I was not going to injure myself or wear myself out on cup final day. Cue more office banter.

We all arrived at Clifton a few hours before kick off because we didn't want to have to rush the warm up or do anything differently to what we usually did on a Saturday. We got ourselves kitted up and went out to the back of the changing rooms on to pitches and areas of playing fields where we could warm up. At any other ground you just warmed up on the pitch, Clifton of course had a separate area for that.

During the warm up we knew we would be interrupted to have our photographs taken with both the winners cup and the runners up. It may seem odd to do this before the game had been played but trying to get a Rugby team to pose for an official photo after the whistle would be like trying to get a group of Welshman to sing swing low.

As it was the final there was absolutely no need for any extra motivation, however we were provided it when we were told that Old C's had refused to have their photo taken with the runners up trophy. Now I'm all for being confident, and in sport I believe that some of the best players in every sport need a touch of arrogance but there is a time and a place, this wasn't it.

We should have been the favourites going into the game being a division higher than Old C's but they had stormed the division below and were beating teams comfortably, so it had the makings for a great match. It was close to kick off, and though there was a definite nervous atmosphere, nerves were good; everyone knew what they had to do and were determined to go out and do it.

We had the two-minute knock from the referee. It was time. Captain for the day and Fly Half Mike Weaver led the team out in front of what was the biggest crowd I had ever played in front of, the Clifton stands were full and the whole of Frampton had come to support us. Some of my mates were watching me play Rugby for the first time; even my Mum and Grandmothers were there!

The game started at a hundred mile an hour with play going back and forth and no one really taking the advantage. Old C's were determined to throw the ball around from anywhere on the pitch however our defence was standing firm and the gain line was barely breached.

Following a failed Old C's attack, Fly Half Weaves cleared the ball from inside the twenty-two but failed to find touch. I chased the ball up the pitch in order to close down the space and as I got closer to their full back I lined him up ready to make the hit. Bang. Down I went. I had positioned my head in the wrong place to make the tackle and the full backs knee caught me just under the left eye. I remember having the all important magic sponge and cold water being poured over my face, there were a few stars but I was running on pure adrenaline and there was nothing that was going to drag me off the pitch that day.

During the first twenty minutes of the match Weaves had nailed two important penalty kicks to give us a small advantage, and at the same time their Fly Half couldn't hit a cows ass with a banjo. As the first half was coming to a close we applied pressure deep in to the Old C's half. First second row Posh John had a try disallowed for an alleged forward pass, but we still pressed on looking for that try.

At this moment I would just like to issue an apology as this part of the story is about to be very self-indulgent.

We had possession just inside the twenty-two on the left hand side, and there were only moments to go in the first half. Rocco, the scrum half passed from the base of a ruck from left to right and hit one of the forward runners to try to set up a quick ball; none were coming. From the following ruck the ball found Weaves, and as Weaves was a sizeable Fly Half, he too attacked the gain line and recycled the ball for Rocco.

I was now standing in the first receiver position and looked right to survey my options; they had numbers there in defence. I dropped deeper to receive the ball from Rocco and line up a drop goal. As the ball came to me the defence rushed up to block the kick, however the kick was never in my mind. I had noticed the dead ball area at Clifton was larger than at most grounds and it could be used to my advantage. I dummied the kick, stepped right, chipped over the on rushing defence, and ran through and collected the ball before diving over the line underneath the posts. It was without doubt the most important and best try I had ever and will ever score. Weaves kicked the simple conversion and we went in at half time in front.

The try that I had just scored was a perfect example of another one of Weaves favourite Rugby quotes. "There was the player that made it happen, there is the player that saw it happen, and there is the player that said what happened?"

Self indulgence over.

The message from the coaches was more of the same, we weren't allowing the Old C's backs to play by rushing and stopping them at source and the forwards were using their physical dominance to take control up front.

The second half was a nervy affair with Old C's finally getting back in to the game as their kicker remembered how to kick and slotted over a few penalties of his own. We then very nearly shot ourselves in the foot when again we were camped in their twenty two and the ball came back to Mike Weaver who had a shout at a drop goal. I think after the Mr Wilkinson incident in Australia everyone was quite keen to emulate him! Weaves was in the pocket, the ball came back and then he sliced the ball so badly it ended up closer to the touch flag than it did the posts. To make matters worse it landed in the hands of one of the Old C's backs, who set off down the pitch at a rate of knots. Thankfully we had our own flyer, Adam Lees, who managed to catch him before he entered our twenty-two, and then with the added weight of Weaves who I had never seen move so fast bundled him into touch. Adam was the only person I know that would bring his sprinting blocks to sports day. He had serious gas.

There were only moments to go in the final, the result was pretty much guaranteed but we weren't finished yet. The Fram forwards continued to grunt, huff and puff in close quarters and we were soon only five meters from the try line. Scrum half Rocco picked up from the ruck and shot through a gap - try time. Cue the celebrations. Frampton were the 2003/04 Charles Saunders Combination Cup Champions.

In the bar the drinks were flowing, songs were sung, and everyone was in very high spirits. It was my first taste of success with Fram and I was enjoying it. The night continued its pattern back in Frampton and as memory recollects there was even a drunken game of naked table Football, again this will be due to Tony Williams.

At the end of the night my girlfriend took me back to her house to stay there. I was definitely worse for wear and feeling a little bit dazed. This may have been the adrenaline finally wearing out and the bump to my head taking affect, I wasn't sure. As with any drunken night I soon passed out within thirty seconds of my head hitting the pillow.

I would now like to make another apology to my ex girlfriend and her parents as I don't think they know what I'm about to write.

As explained I went to bed rather dazed. The next thing I remember is waking up in the middle of the night and going to toilet in my girlfriend's kitchen. I have no recollection of how I got there but I do remember waking up very quickly after and thinking shit, what have I done! Luckily the floor was vinyl and therefore wipeable, all I needed to do now was clean up before anyone else woke up! I found the kitchen roll and got to work, five minutes, later mission accomplished no one would ever know, (until I decided to write a book!) and I went back to bed, though now with a splitting headache.

When I finally woke up the following morning, in bed this time, not in the kitchen, I had the world's worst hangover but this was no normal hangover my head was pounding. As I began to get showered and dressed I noticed something wasn't quite right with my face, not with the look of it, I was still a handsome bugger, but the feel of it. Then I realised what it was; I had no feeling in my face from below my left eye to my top lip. This was not good, though it did give me a sort of excuse for the kitchen incident.

I got myself ready, rang the old man and off we went to the hospital. After the standard three-hour wait I had some tests and an x-ray. Luckily nothing was broken though I had nerve damage, the feeling in the side of my face would come back over time but for a while there would be nothing. The other upside to this kind of injury meant I didn't have to have a break from playing Rugby.

All in all it had been a successful season, we had made progression in the league, we had won the cup and as a squad we were gaining more strength in depth with a small influx of South Africans. To finish off the season there was still a small tour to Cork to be enjoyed.

The tour to Cork was another two-night trip leaving early on the Friday morning. We were flying from Cardiff and as a result it was an early morning coach trip to the airport. Again the air was filled with excitement of men being allowed to fend for themselves on a weekend away.

After the customary pint in the airport at a time when alcohol should not be consumed it was time to board the plane. I was sat next to big Pete Zaffiro, a stalwart of the club and someone who when you looked at them wouldn't be phased by much. Unfortunately for him and me this was not the case. Poor old Zaff did not like flying, and with me being the young pup sat next to him, I was to hold his hand. His grip was like a vice I was going nowhere! As you can imagine the rest of the touring party were very sympathetic to Zaff's fear of flying.

The theme for the tour was handbags and hats, and at all times you had to ensure you had 3 items in your handbag that a woman would carry around with them. This was obviously open to interpretation and there were all sorts of items brought. In fact I think with the items we had on tour we could have hosted our own Ann Summers party.

The tour was another great weekend away with the boys, and the Irish were all very accommodating - we even managed to win our tour game. In the airport on the way home just as we were going through the security check one of the handbag items, which we shall call "Rubber Justice", found its way in to Rocco's coat. We had already tipped off the airport security as to what we had done and asked them to pull him over. After ensuring Rocco was last to go through the gates we all stood at the one end and watched in delight as "Rubber Justice" was pulled from his coat and pointed at Rocco, while the security guard questioned what Rocco's intentions were. Priceless.

What on earth is a Kudu?

It was around Christmas time during my last year in University and it was time to start applying for jobs as the 2 shifts a week at Pizza Hut weren't going to justify my 4 years at Uni. After applying for numerous accounting firms and a couple of interviews I was offered a role for Grant Thornton in Cheltenham and would start in the September.

Back on the Rugby field Frampton had begun to benefit from their mini influx of friends from South Africa, mainly from the Morsner Clan. The first player to join us was a number 8 by the name of Dean Morsner. Dean was a sizeable lad standing at around 6ft 4 with strawberry blonde hair and weighing around 18stone. Suddenly our five-metre scrum became a very potent weapon!

Dean being the first team number 8 however did mean we encountered some language issues around some of our calls. One such call was an "animal" ball where from a scrum the ball is passed from the scrum half to the Fly Half who then runs a switch with the number 8 who in theory should be crashing in to a much smaller Fly Half.

During one match we had a scrum in the middle of the field; Deano looks at Weaves and calls a Kudu ball. From the scrum Rocco passes the ball to Weaves who then sends a kick to the corner leaving Deano in the middle of his run looking dumbfounded.

"I called a Kudu ball, what are you doing!!"
"What on earth is bloody Kudu?"
"It's an animal, like a Springbok..!"
"How the fuck am I meant to know that?"

The next South African to join us was Dean's brother Dwayne, another giant who would bulk up the second row. Dwayne was a fiery character who liked to voice his opinion. One training session we backs split from the forwards so we could go and practice our moves and looking good whilst the forwards could practice their grunting.

As we were in the middle of a passing drill there was a noise from the forwards layer and a scuffle broke out with Dwayne and Mike Prosser being held apart by the other forwards. First instinct was to run over and help out, though the closer you get to the forwards the larger they become, and on second glance it was decided it was probably best to let them sort this one out themselves. It was no place for a back.

The final member of the Morsner clan to join the Fram was Mark Kane, Dean's cousin. Mark was only 18 when he joined but looked about ten years older. Mark would occupy the back row with his cousin and the ever present and ever impressive Keith Weaver.

It was evident from the first game that Mark was a different class; by about the third game of the season the bookies had stopped taking bets on who would win player of the season at the annual dinner. Another plus point of having Mark in the back row meant that I didn't have to tackle nearly as much as I used to, which in turn helped preserve my looks.

The end of the season was near and as I was in my last year at university I made the sensible decision not to tour as I had exams to study for; the boys were off to Chester and I was gutted to be missing out.

During the summer we had the misfortune of entering a couple of sevens tournaments. Sevens was not a form of the game we practiced, ever, and if you watched us on a Saturday this was no surprise given our hefty pack. Assembling a squad for such events was never easy, especially given not many people enjoyed the event and it was outside the season when the majority of the club's players were either on holiday, playing cricket, or just not allowed to play as the boss (wife) said so.

With most sevens teams you base your team around some very fast players and then include the more mobile of the forwards, who may even be your larger backs. For us this was not the case, our team was purely based on who was available on the weekend. This weekend the answer was not a lot!

Aside from a sevens team from the pacific islands we were possibly entering a sevens tournament with the heaviest team on record. The team included Captain Paul (ex para and front row), the South African pairing of Deano and Mark (combined weight = fat), Posh John (big Scottish second row), Tom Bass (angry ginger flanker) and thankfully a few backs. Looking at the squad however there was no doubting that we would not be looking to play the normal style of sevens…the more contact the better.

The tournament started surprisingly well and after the first two matches we were sitting top of our pool having won both games. Even more surprisingly the tournament continued in the same vein and we soon found ourselves the Bristol Imperial 7s tournament winners!

The key to our success so far was where most teams were full of smaller flyers and we had heavier lumpers, the smaller flyers weren't too keen on tackling the likes of Posh John and Deano and if they did finally bring them down it took 2 or 3 of them. With it being 7 a side it did leave a lot of room for the few backs we did have to run in the tries.

In theory this should have been a one off, and it is no surprise that the 7s circuit continues to be dominated by teams with skill and pace, however the following year we managed to retain the title in very similar circumstances! A triumph for the fatties!.

Most successes in the club were followed up with a night out, not that the majority of the boys needed an excuse, but a night out was planned and it was again a walk round the village after a few beers at the club. When a night is planned there are always a few characters in the club, and I'm sure it's the same all over the country, that like to perform. Frampton's performer was Wayne Kay, or Wayner, as is the more Bristolian way.

Wayner is probably the closest thing Frampton has to a celebrity in that he has performed as Grizzly Bear (Bristol Rugby Club mascot), was frequently phoned up by the local radio station for his views on the a nature of topics, and is a one man entertainment show when on form.

This particular night was also Wayner's birthday and Wayner was on form. First we would see his first party trick: the yard of ale. Now everyone knows someone that can down a pint and down it quickly, however this man was a machine. In fact he was better than a machine; he had beat machines (an industrial vacuum in a drink off on tour).

As the news spread around the club that Wayne was about to do his yard of ale a crowd soon gathered, it was something that everyone wanted to see. Many had seen it before but it was like watching a live version of record breakers, and something you would never be tired of watching. Like with any drink off the chorus of "Why was he born so beautiful" was started and then a few seconds later it was over. The yard was seen off in around 7 seconds.

This talent of Wayne's had been used to the clubs advantage, especially on Rugby tours. On one such tour, after the customary match you are forced to play on tour, we were back in the opposition clubhouse enjoying the festivities when we were challenged to a boat race. We had to send our 4 best drinkers up to face the challenge that was thrown down. We sent Wayne. Just Wayne. They questioned our logic saying there was no way that one man could beat their team of 4.

"On your marks, Get set, Go…" The opposition second man was merely half way through his pint as Wayne finished his fourth. We knew it was going to happen, but it was still a sight to behold.

Wayne liked to have a sing, and after finishing off his yard of ale it was time to perform his second party piece, "The Wanderer by Dion". When Wayne is about to sing you know exactly what song it's going to be, as I'm pretty sure he only knows the words to one song, but he has it nailed and even performs the instrumental. And thanks to Wayne I, along with most of Frampton also now know the words:

Oh well, I'm the type of guy who will never settle down
Where pretty girls are well, you know that I'm around
I kiss 'em and I love 'em 'cause to me they're all the same
I hug 'em and I squeeze 'em they don't even know my name

They call me the wanderer

Yeah, the wanderer
I roam around, around, around....

The new season had started and I was now working up in Cheltenham for GT whilst still living at home with my parents in Bristol. The commute was around an hour, though as long as I left on time I was still able to make training on Tuesday and Thursday. In my first year however I had to spend a lot of time working away in High Wycombe, probably around three months between September and Christmas. Needless to say spending time on a residential course, with nothing to do but drink, with some token training thrown in, I may have started my transition to a crash ball centre.

My weeks started to develop a pattern where I would travel up to High Wycombe on a Sunday evening, travel back on a Friday night, then Saturday I'd play Rugby and see the girlfriend under duress as I had to leave the drinking at the Rugby club, and then on Sunday head back up to High Wycombe. Unsurprisingly this began to take its toll on my relationship and it wasn't long before we split.

The timing of the split was not the greatest (although when are they?) As the following weekend I was to attend a charity event with my ex-girlfriend which she had helped organise with a partner of another Frampton player. Unfortunately it was not just my ex-girlfriend that was going, there were also her parents, her sister, and her auntie and uncle. This had the potential to be very awkward though it was for a good cause and I had promised to support her so as they say "the show must go on". As the evening progressed and the drink consumption increased the evening began to be a little awkward; luckily there was the saving grace that as the event was organised by a couple of WAGS of the Rugby club there was a strong contingent of the team present. Like any good team when they see a member is struggling they step in to help them out, and that is exactly what happened to me.

Big Nathan Cole could see I was struggling and told me to come to the bar with him. This is where we stayed for the rest of the evening, I had no idea how the rest of the evening panned out but I do know from my head the next morning it must have been a good one.

Spending the amount of time I did in High Wycombe it was no surprise that relationships started and I soon become very friendly with a small Welsh girl named Gemma. Now Gemma wasn't my usual type in that she was Welsh - but other than that she was perfect. A proper little (5ft) stunner, and the more time I spent with her I realised the Welsh thing wasn't that bad. For one she didn't have an accent so I didn't have to tell people, she knew an awful lot about Rugby, especially for a girl, and there was someone instantly available to take the mick out of come international weekends.

One such international weekend was coming up when Wales was playing South Africa and England was playing New Zealand. However the matches this weekend would play second fiddle to Jack Russell's stag do. In order to celebrate all the boys were heading over to the Welsh capital for a day and night on the tiles.

A number of the boys were taking the train across and catching the last train back, however our first team Fly Half Matt Lawrence had just started university in Cardiff and had asked me and Ginger Jonesy to crash at his place so I was going to drive over.

As I was driving I offered a lift to anyone that wanted one and the first people to take me up on the offer were, Smither (6ft2, 18stone), Deano (6ft4, 18 stone), Mark Kane (6ft2, 16 stone) and Weaves (6ft2, 16 stone) along with my slender self my poor car was in for a hell of a beating. At the time I was only driving a Citroen Saxo not a car built for that kind of punishment and since the journey to Cardiff my car was never the same again and it wasn't long before it retired to the scrap heap.

We arrived in Cardiff, dropped my stuff off with Matt and all headed for the pub where there was a section reserved for Jack's stag. The boys had turned out in good numbers and the bar was already brimming. The first game of the day was England vs. the All Blacks and as soon as the national anthems started we were soon reminded where we were as a chorus of Land of my Fathers broke out and the banter started. There is nowhere else like Wales in the world on match day, it really is a religion.

During the game Gemma and a few friends walked in to the bar, and I know it's bad form to have your misses turn up on a boys night out but as none of the lads had met her before they had no idea she was actually my misses and just thought I had done well during the day!

Within ten minutes of meeting the lads she had been asked by Weaves if she had seen it or touched it first and she replied without batting an eye lid - and then sat on Deano's shoulders so she could see the game. This girl was looking like a keeper.

As the England game came to an end, a few of us that had tickets headed for the Stadium to watch the game; if nothing else it was a couple of hours break from the constant drinking in the bar. The game was close though at the end, it was Deano and Mark that were the happiest.

Back in the bar the pace had really stepped up and Frampton's flash harry (Chris Bray) had begun to play his part. Usually the promotional drinks girls have to work to sell the shots but with Chris on form there was no need and it was a great way to play catch up. From then on in the night took its usual course of drinks, more drinks, club, and kebab and finally back to Mr Lawrence's digs.

I was awoken in the morning to Ginger Jonesy arriving in the kitchen, where for some reason I had decided to sleep, in Matt's flat mates pink dressing gown. It was a sight to behold and after meeting Gemma earlier that evening not something I had hoped or thought I would be waking up to see.

Trips to Cardiff became a bit more frequent with Matt Lawrence having student accommodation there, and we soon made sure that when Wales were playing on a Friday night, usually against one of the Pacific island teams, we would pick up cheap tickets and head on over. The usual suspects for a night away were myself, Ginger Jonesy, Eddy (it's not the Netherlands it's Holland) Barrett who had come back from university and was now playing for us, and Joe Bennett.

Joe was a confident lad around the ladies and always claimed that if he had my height he would make a killing. One example of Joe's confidence was when we were in the car on the way to Cardiff and we were stuck in a traffic queue. Joe had noticed a car full of young ladies in the car in front and decided to try his luck. He wrote down his phone number on a piece of paper, and bold as brass walked up to the car in front, knocked on the window, handed over the piece of paper and said "I'm fit and so are you so give me a call sometime". It would have worked if knocking on the window hadn't surprised the girls so much that it caused them to stall the car. But it was a prime example of the attitude and motto: if you throw enough shit, some will eventually stick.

Matt however was a different kind of character and had a very different approach to Joe. In fact they were polar opposites. Matt was the type of guy who liked the women to do all the work, now for someone like me this would be pointless as I would just be standing and waiting for a very long time. Matt however, and it pains me to say this, had that boy band look about him, and he knew it.

There were countless occasions where on a night out girls made it painfully obvious to Matt they were interested in him and he just completely blanked them or paid no interest whatsoever. This infuriated Joe and I, probably as we had very rarely had the same type of attention, and it just fuelled Matt's ego.

Just to add more fuel to the burning furnace that was Matt's ego he was also stopped in a well-known dimly lit, music blaring, very trendy American fashion store and asked if he had ever considered modelling, and on a separate occasion followed around a Supermarket by an attractive professional lady and then given her business card as he sat in his car eating lunch. It never happens to me!

The trips to Cardiff were always good fun though maybe sometimes a little mistimed. On one occasion we travelled back to Frampton on the Saturday feeling a little worse for wear and having to play a potentially tough game against the monsters from Bream. We were in contention for promotion and this was a game we really couldn't afford to lose. Luckily for us, and for me, Bream were not good travellers and quite often you would play a different team at home compared to when playing them away. During the warm up I was still wasn't feeling 100% so disappeared for a tactical chunder to try to perk myself up. This seemed to have the desired effect as we won the game comfortably and no one was the wiser.

During the season the club had brought in fitness coach Mark Hammond to whip the boys into shape and keep them in shape during the season. No small task. It was the first time that a coach had been brought in to specifically concentrate on fitness. With Marks professional knowledge and expertise the fitness training changed dramatically, it was position specific, stretches were now dynamic and all the boys really embraced the change. Even the fatties.

We were now seeing more people training on a Tuesday than ever before, and even seeing some of the old boys coming out of the woodwork. During the winter months when the weather causes training to be cancelled we now had Mark taking boxercise classes in the community centre. We were fast becoming one of the fittest sides in the league and as a result becoming one of the strongest sides in Gloucester One, so it was time for that promotion push.

Before the start of the new season it was time for the annual tour, but it wouldn't be the usual tour, we would be visiting a club we had close links to and enjoyed a cross channel relationship with - we were off to France to be hosted by Parisis.

The majority of interaction between the two clubs was done between the junior section and the Vets (or Old Gits as they were affectionately known) but this time we were taking over a full senior compliment. Although touring to France was exciting and something different it did have one major downside, a bloody long coach journey!

We met in Crossbow car park at the unpleasant time of 6am all dressed in our berets and stripy jumpers, excited about a weekend away. No matter what the hour at the start of a Rugby tour, a beer is always enjoyed. The only variable seemed to be the type of food you had with it, and in this case it was a bacon roll.

The beer continued to flow as we travelled across country to catch the cross channel ferry and by the time we boarded the boat we were all very well lubricated. The tour slaves had now been kitted out with their fancy dress attire and Ginger Rob Cobley was looking very fetching as Dorothy from the Wizard of Oz. Once aboard the boat we all headed for the bar, probably due to its magnetic field, for another pint.

As it was March 17th we decided that everyone should have a Guinness in order to celebrate our Celtic neighbour's Patron Saint's day. Also on tour was Josh Kohn. Josh is your typical old school front row forward who doesn't believe in fitness; his idea of a warm up is to have a cigarette, and a nutritious pre match meal consists of a pie. Yet he was only 20 years old. It was like he was born 30 years too late, and even at 20 had that old man strength.

Josh being very old school also fully believed that slaves were there to be abused and were solely there for his entertainment. Believing this Josh ordered Rob a straight quadruple Gin. Now this wouldn't be seen as complete abuse but given that it was still before 9 in the morning and we had a long way to go, the more senior party members told Josh that at the very least he had to let Rob have a mixer with his drink. Without hesitation Josh grabbed Rob's Gin, and poured his Guinness in to the drink and with that the Giness cocktail was born. Surprisingly it hasn't caught on.

We arrived on French soil and still had a long way to go. It wasn't until around 10pm that we arrived at Parisis Rugby club. We were met with excitement and great hospitality, before being paired up with our hosts for the weekend.

My host was there with his girlfriend and seemed to be a lot more reserved than the majority of the hosts but still seemed pleasant enough. I was taken back to his parents' house to meet the family where they had prepared a meal with some expensive French red wine. Meeting and staying with a foreign family for the first time, when dressed in a beret, stripy jumper and having been on the beers for over 12 hours wasn't an ideal scenario but using my GCSE/Del Boy French I think I managed to impress.

After dinner I was expecting to be able to go to bed as it was close to midnight; I had been up since 5, drinking since 6 and somehow was expected to play Rugby the following day. The host however had other plans and we were soon back in his car heading back to the Rugby club where we met with the rest of the touring party (well those that were under 30) and then boarded a coach.

The coach journey seemed like an eternity before we arrived at what looked like a warehouse where they were playing Euro dance music. When we entered the locals didn't seem too enthralled by having a load of drunken English Rugby players turn up, but to be fair, who would!

As well as having a dance floor and a chill out area the "club" also had a room with a swimming pool. Given that it was March, the pool wasn't heated and it was around 2 in the morning so it was no surprise that the locals steered clear of the pool. We however were not locals and after a bit of "shall we shan't we" were soon jumping in the pool with our French hosts close behind.

We soon decided enough was enough in the pool - it became clear why there were no locals in the pool - it was freezing! On top of this I was now beyond shattered but the coach wasn't due to leave for another hour, so I decided the best idea was to chill out for an hour and sit on one of the sofas. Rocco happened to have the same idea as me at the same time. An hour later we were both woken up whist spooning and told the bus was about to leave. At least we were warm!

The next day I woke up with the usual tour hangover, though instead of the usual full English and a pint, there were fresh croissants, cold ham, cheeses and a selection of fruit juices. This tour was definitely different.

We headed to the Rugby club where the pitch was bathed in sunshine but given the way everyone looked and felt after the previous day's festivities, this was going to be hard work. However unlike any other tour match, there was more than just local pride at stake, there was national pride - we were playing for England. My host was not playing today as him and his girlfriend were off looking at houses. Convenient excuse.

The anthems took place and we were ready for kick off. The match was intense with neither side wanting to lose. The Parisis team was made up of a large number of their Vets due to their first fifteen having a league fixture. This was just as well as we had rather an eclectic mix of tourists and would have been soundly beaten had we had to play the first team.

We were soon under the cosh due to some rather dodgy home refereeing but with the trusty boot of Mike Weaver we were never out of reach and the lead went back and forth during a tight first half. During the second half we began to take control as the French Vets started to find the pace of the game under the Parisian sun a bit much and with tries from Chaps and I we ran out comfortable winners.

After the game the Parisis team continued to be the perfect hosts as we were taken to a hotel where a function room was hired for the evening. There was one of the best buffets I have ever seen accompanied by copious amounts of booze. During the night there was a couple of presentations and thank yous. Chaps, presenting on behalf of the Fram, delivered one of the best speeches I have ever heard, not in content but for pure comedy value. It was a mixture of French, English and then made up French words by adding letters on to the end of words, and with it being Chaps it was generally expletives. The highlight was without doubt when he called their club captain a "Bastardo!"

The one downside about a tour in Paris is the journey back on the Sunday; everyone is feeling rough from the night before and everyone just wants to be home. We were however entertained by this year's slaves during their naked swim. Somewhere on a French highway behind a service station there was a river and the slaves were ordered off and stripped to perform their swim. You could tell by the look on their faces and the funny shade of blue they all went that it was cold. This was noticed by Josh Kohn who quickly, well quickly for Josh, ran to the shop and bought them all an ice cream. He really is all heart.

Par Avion

It was the start of a new season and one of Frampton's old boys was back to take charge: Sean Hodges aka, Reggie. Reggie was known as much for his Rugby as he was for his off field antics, especially on Sodbury high street.

We started the season in great form reaping the rewards from a full pre-season with Mark Hammond. We were fitter than every team we came up against and were playing a lot more expansive Rugby. Sides couldn't cope with us and by Christmas it was a two horse race for the title.

The season however was not all plain sailing, and for me personally was also bloody painful. It was a cold wet Saturday in November, not that Saturdays in November are any different, but I'd thought I would set the scene. We were playing home against Gloucester Old Boys up at Hooper's Farm instead of the usual Stade de Crossbow and the game was going well. We were twenty minutes in and already in the ascendancy.

Gloucester Old Boys had the ball and sent their inside centre up the middle, I stepped in to make the tackle, which was probably Matt Lawrence's to make, my head was the wrong side and crack… knee in the side of the face. I tried to shake it off, bit of cold water and I carried on, things seemed a bit fuzzy but I thought I would be alright. Five minutes later we were awarded a scrum, a simple miss two was called. The ball would be passed to me and I would pass to the fullback missing out my outside centre. Unfortunately the ball came to me and I dropped it. Now I don't usually make many excuses but I genuinely had one this time, I didn't see the ball!

I came off the pitch and headed for the hospital, obviously not being able to see properly was a bit of an issue in terms of driving though as my Dad watches every game, I was sure he would take me. Wrong, both he and Grandad stood on the side of the pitch and said, ring Gem she will take you. Any other day Gem would have also been on the side of the pitch watching the Rugby what with her being Welsh. However it was also my sister Holly's 21st birthday so she was busy helping the Mother Ship do some prepping in the kitchen.

Three hours in A&E and then a further hour in the eye hospital and I was back home ready to celebrate my sister's birthday, unfortunately with a fractured eye socket but luckily no detached retina as was feared. I did however resemble Sloth from the Goonies as my face had dropped on one side. Heeey Yooouuuuu Guyyssss!

This injury had its plus points; it wasn't going to stop me from keeping fit, it guaranteed me a week off work, and the games I would be missing would be in December and January which are not the greatest months to play in the backs. Soft backs or intelligent, you decide?

The weeks on the sidelines did mean I could have some spare time on a Saturday afternoon, though I was far too young for Garden centres, didn't like shopping and was useless at DIY so the only thing to do was to come along and watch Frampton carry on their winning ways.

After the couple of months on the side I was soon back in the mix, and looking forward to the end of the season run in. Promotion was almost certainly guaranteed but it was looking like it would come down to a home fixture against our local rivals Chipping Sodbury.

In previous seasons, fixtures against Sodbury had always been fiercely fought contests. This season however was different as we were flying high and they were languishing at the bottom of the league; surely there could only be one winner. But this was a local derby, pride was at stake, form went out the window, this was a match that no one could predict...

That's enough of the build up trying to make it sound like a close encounter, it wasn't. We absolutely trounced them; it was one of the most convincing wins of the season. Prolific winger and nudist Tony Williams scored a brace to yet again be the team's top try scorer and even veteran Fly Half Mike Weaver rolled back the years to cross the white wash along with the equally old ex Bristol utility back Barry Whitehead.

As well as a successful season in the league we had yet again reached the Charles Saunders cup final, and would be facing Gordano. The long season, although successful, had taken its toll and come cup final day there were a number of first team regulars who were missing with injuries. It was going to be an uphill battle but this was a cup final and anything could happen.

Come cup final day Gordano were just too strong for us and their added experience proved vital. Also the mercurial Fly Half Matt Lawrence had a day to forget with the boot. If anything the final showed us that even though we had been promoted we had plenty to work on if we were to survive in the upper leagues.

The end of the season saw the return visit of the Parisis team to Frampton and the boys had plenty planned for our French visitors including making sure we kept up our winning record against them on the pitch.

The first meeting with our French counterparts was at Crossbow where we would find out which player we had been assigned for the weekend. As I was still living at home I kindly offered up a room at my parent's house, and as my Mum took A level French I was sure they wouldn't mind.

When they arrived and were making their way off the coach into the club house there were definitely a number of them that I was hoping I didn't have to take back to meet my parents as they were feeling the effects of a 15 hour Rugby coach journey! Luckily I struck gold. I was given my opposite number, the only touring member who didn't drink! Rather embarrassingly I have forgotten his name but for the sake of this book we will call him Pascal. On the plus side Pascal would be no trouble whatsoever, on the downside I was soon being told he was like hot shit off a shovel and would spend all day tomorrow running around me, and this was even more likely given the fact he would not be hung-over! I had to come up with a plan.

After a few pints at the club with a 'get to know your guests' evening the morning of the game was soon upon us. For the morning I had planned to show Pascal the sites of Bristol and give him an English experience. Firstly we set off to the town Centre where we had a look round the S.S. Great Britain, climbed Cabot Tower and took him to see the Suspension Bridge; all within about thirty minutes. And there were other things that I was determined for him to experience. Firstly a pint of proper cider from the Llandogger Trow, Bristol's oldest pub and then more importantly a full English. Hopefully this would slow him down!

On the way back from town we stopped in the lay by on the Badminton Road and I ordered him the Belly Buster. There were whimpers of protest but if the boy wasn't going to drink I was making sure he was going to eat. I had no intention of chasing a French 21 year old's shadow around all afternoon. I decided against ordering anything for myself and just stood there and watched him eat, making sure nothing was left.

The game itself was a bruiser with Frampton probably benefiting from some home refereeing but a win was a win and more importantly the flying Frenchman didn't score or go round me. Ashwin 1, Pascal 0.

I had organised the evening's entertainment for our guests which would be taking place at the local Cricket club which may have been an unusual choice of venue but it was strategically chosen given that it was free and out in the sticks where we would not be disturbed.

Through a friend's uncle I had organised a "Gentleman's" evening, though this could be more accurately described as a night with two strippers. With the risk of making the book x rated, I will just provide a few ingredients and you can build your own story...

- Copious amounts of beer
- Squirty cream
- Marshmallows
- 2 strippers
- Blindfolds
- An angry barmaid
- Thrown water
- And a lot of happy Frenchman.

Whatever story you have just concocted you are probably not far off the truth. On the Sunday morning we packed Pascal off with an English picnic and sent him on the bus on the way home. A successful weekend.

There was one more twist to the French visit that I hadn't foreseen as over the weekend I had managed to "lose" my kitbag. Although I was convinced I had left it in the trunk in the changing room I was being told that it had "probably" been misplaced and put on the French coach with the rest of the bags. I could smell a stitch up.

Sure enough come the annual dinner and the award for Plank of the year coming up, my name was announced and I was presented my kit bag in a large box with a "par avion" sticker and inside my bag was onions, garlic and French cheese. It hummed!

The annual dinner was also a memorable night for me in that I picked up my 200 badge. A badge that indicated I had played in 200 games for the club. Only a handful of players have picked up this badge and I am privileged to say I am one of them. There are members of the club that have played over 700 games for the club... and some of those are also life sponsors of Deep Heat.

The Welsh adventure

Promotion to the Gloucester Premiership saw the introduction of a forwards coach, Lee Ashford, to help out Reggie. Lee was affectionately known as Mighty Mouse and had played the majority of his Rugby for Clifton in the front row and was definitely in the old school mould of forwards. No more so was this the case when we were running through one of his drills called "dull fuckers" (where you run a gauntlet and get smashed).

On a personal note Gemma and I had decided to take the plunge and buy a house. I really should have paid more attention in this process as I actually bought the house without seeing it and was told by Gem by text that she had bought one while I was playing cricket! And that it was in WALES! I wasn't sure I would be accepted back at Frampton, or even back with my family! However the decision to continue to play for Frampton and commute on a Thursday and Saturday to train and play helped with the transition.

The first season in the Gloucester Premiership saw us travelling up the M5 to play against teams we had not encountered before in the lower leagues; teams such as Old Richians, Drybrook and Matson. Although these teams tended to be a lot stronger on their own patch compared to when you got them out of Gloucester. On one such occasion we travelled up the M5 and were on the end of a proper hiding from Matson who were well drilled and very physical. It was also quite an intimidating place to go, made even more so by the scenes of crime vehicles in the road approaching the club where there had been a stabbing the night before.

The one thing however that was enjoyable about the trip to Matson was the old style Rugby bath they had in the changing rooms; these were not usually seen anymore with all clubs having the communal showers. What made the Rugby bath more enjoyable was the fact we managed to persuade Leslie our physio to join us.

In the return fixture when we had Matson down at Stadio de Crossbow it was a completely different game, probably because Matson brought down a completely different team, which may have been because of work commitments but also could be due to players not being allowed to leave a certain mile radius from their house for the danger of their tag going off.

The game was evenly balanced coming up to the end of the first half when Frampton trundled over with a typical catch and drive from a lineout when suddenly the forward handbags started flying. As a centre I decided watching was a better option. After the melee had calmed down Matson had 2 players sent off and one sin binned, Frampton had just the one in the bin. This wouldn't have been a huge issue but of the 3 people that Matson had lost, 2 were in the front row and one in the second row.

The following scrum was one of the most one-sided contests you would have ever witnessed. Matson bodies were left scattered. One of the more experienced Matson players had had enough, his shirt was coming off and he said, I quote, "f*ck this, I've got to go to work tomorrow, I've had enough". The rest of his team followed him and the match was abandoned.

As well as now living in Wales I had just moved jobs and was beginning to work in Wales in the picturesque town of

Newport for Tata Steel works. And as if I couldn't get enough of Wales this year's tour was also in Wales and more precisely in Tenby.

I and the ever-present fullback Simon Belston had worked hard booking a hotel and arranging a fixture on both the Saturday and Sunday for the boys, as well as a well-deserved pub stop in Newcastle Emlyn en route to Tenby. The tour theme for the year was Country Gents with the tour slaves kitted out as farmyard animals.

We arrived at the hotel and after some "random" room picking I was walking up to my room with Joe Bennett. As we were walking along the corridor we could hear a noisy group of girls who all sounded very excited to be away for the weekend, and not being shy I knocked on the door and introduced myself and kindly asked if they could keep the noise down as Joe and I had come for a nice quiet weekend away. Joe looked horrified, and asked what on earth I had done that for... I told him to wait....

Two minutes later there was a knock on our door and the same group of girls were introducing themselves to us and apologising for the noise. Joe was very quick to explain we were winding them up and were in fact on a Rugby tour. A few eyebrows rose. We were soon back in their room enjoying a drink and waving down to the fellow Gents of the tour party who had frequented in the beer garden and couldn't believe our luck!

We soon made our excuses and left to get involved in the serious drinking. We did however send one of our slaves, who will remain unnamed, up to say hello to our new friends from Merthyr Tydfil; he returned later rather flushed.

The Friday night out in Tenby was a great laugh and we soon found out that the drinking hole that was open the latest was our hotel that had a downstairs bar that doubled up as a nightclub. I'd like to say it was down to mine and Simon's perfect planning but I would be lying. As we entered the hotel bar we again saw our friends from Merthyr who looked like they had not left the hotel bar and had sunk a fair few. The bunch of girls had however doubled in size from when we first met them and we soon found out it was because they had come away for a "bingo" weekend with their Mothers and Aunties!!

Now being a bingo weekend you'd think it would be a fairly tame affair. Oh how wrong you would be! As I was returning from the bar with pints in hand (not sure where my slave was) one of the girls from Merthyr was walking passed me and towards a girl that had just come out of the toilet. One quick tap on the shoulder, a right hook and it was all kicking off – but this was no ordinary cat-fight!! When it all finally calmed down, mostly due to us helping out and not the 2 doormen that were at the hotel, we found out that there had been some "name calling" between the girls from Merthyr and a group from Neath!

The next day we were up and in kangaroo court, firstly to ensure everyone had adhered to the tour theme. As usual it was a cracking effort by everyone, however there was one newcomer on this tour and at the time who was a bit of an unknown quantity. Jon Britton. Jon came up to the honourable Judge Rides and said he had come as a homicidal prostitute sheep, and he wasn't lying. Indeed he had a Sheep mask, stockings and suspenders. It really was a sight to behold. People didn't know whether to laugh or cry, though one thing they were sure they didn't want to happen was to be left alone with him.

We left Tenby and set off for Pembroke Dock to play Rugby. As was the norm with any tour side, we had players playing out of position just to make sure we had a side out. Tours really did bring the non-playing members out for the weekend. I was to play Fly Half. Well I attempted to play Fly Half as my game lasted all of about fifteen minutes as while defending with no one around me I went over on my ankle damaging my ligaments. It was like I had been picked off by a sniper, lying there in a heap.

Back at the hotel my consortium of Wing Commander Badger, Corporal Williams, and Lieutenant Bennett looked after me by finding me a wheelchair. My slave for the day Ashley Weaver also stepped up to the plate and went above and beyond the call of duty. I had asked him to go and get me a bag of ice from behind the bar, and he came back with a nurse who was away for the weekend as well as a bag of ice. Couldn't fault it.

On the Sunday, with sore heads we all set off for Magor to play the one tour game everyone moans about: the second one after the second night before. Everyone accepts having to play one game on the Saturday, but the game on the Sunday is always an enigma to me. Why would you play two games in two days? You don't do it during the normal season yet we decide to do it whilst combining it with two days of non-stop drinking. Luckily or unluckily for me due to my sprained ankle I would be taking no part in the game so would be enjoying a cider in the sun, and I'll be honest, it made my Sunday a lot more enjoyable despite the pain.

Season of injuries

During pre-season we had an arranged friendly match against local rivals Chipping Sodbury. We gave them another absolute tuning, like we did to gain promotion the previous season. We ran riot, scoring tries for fun, dominating in both the forwards and the backs, and on the hard summer ground our running Rugby really did look impressive and was a solid platform to launch the season. I however did not have that much luck, as while I was tackled I placed my hand down to break my fall and broke my scaphoid, which meant I would be out for a couple of months and all my pre-season work would be undone.

The season saw the introduction of Chalky as the head coach, and was the first time that the club had brought in a coach from outside the club to pick up the reigns. Chalky's appointment brought with it a new way of thinking and gone was the old mentality of being guaranteed a game because of who you were, and that certain players had certain positions.

This included me and after a couple of games back from my return from the wrist injury I was being asked to play full back instead of the centre. The reasons being was that I could kick, was fairly safe under the high ball and when I did come in to the line given my size (I was now definitely a crash ball centre) I would break some holes in the opposition defence. The first game I was asked to play was a midweek game under lights in wet conditions, not ideal.

The game didn't start well as I dropped the first two balls that were kicked to me (safe hands my arse) but I was blaming the lights and the conditions, not my ability, so carried on still confident that I could do a good job. The next kick that came my way I gathered and set off on a run, but as I looked to step the first defender my ankle turned underneath me, again, and I was down and in pain. This full back lark was not going so well.

It was nights like this that I wish I didn't have the commute back to Wales after each match. On a Saturday it was no issue as Gemma would either come over, watch me play and then dutifully drive me home or we would both have a drink at the club and stay at the olds. However on a wet midweek night with another injured ankle and work the next day the hour drive home was one of the last things I wanted to do.

Being injured is one of the most frustrating things that can happen during the season, I quickly become agitated and as Gemma will confirm very annoying to live with. I need a release of energy and something to get stuck in to. This season for me was pretty much a write off.

One last Season

The commuting was getting to me and it wasn't becoming any easier, it wasn't as easy to stay connected to the club whilst living an hour away, and to make matters worse people were now saying I was developing a welsh accent. I don't know. you call your mate 'butt' once and you are suddenly Welsh.

There had yet again been a change in the coaching regime at Frampton with former captain Paul Beet taking the helm. With Paul came backs coach and scrum half Liam and flanker and fitness Coach Mark. The trio had previously been playing and coaching at Cleve and with any change in regime brings new ideas.

We were struggling with the Fly Half position as Matt Lawrence had gone to ply his trade at Avonmouth; I was filling in as best I could but as people will agree I'm by no means a "natural ten". I was still in touch with Matt and regularly asked how he was getting on at Avonmouth, and it soon transpired that he was being asked to play full back and not getting the game time he was hoping for. Maybe there was a chance he would come back.

I let Paul know and after a few more phone calls Matt was on his way back to Frampton. Or as Matt liked to brand it: "The return of the Messiah". But that was Matt; he fully believed he was Frampton poster boy and our answer to Gavin Henson.

On the pitch it wasn't the most successful of seasons though and at times was very frustrating as things weren't happening for us and we were losing games that we shouldn't have. With the build up of frustration came my most embarrassing moment on a Rugby pitch. We were playing Old Colstonian's and yet again we were losing, nothing was working and I was fed up. I don't know why I did what I did, but after being tackled late, not that late but late, I swung one of the biggest haymakers that has ever been seen. In fact it was so big I think the opposition player saw it coming last Christmas, and if that wasn't bad enough the punch missed by a good 3 feet. I rightly received a yellow card and took my ten minutes under the sticks.

To make things even more embarrassing the attempted punch had been right in front of my Dad, Granddad and a group of my Dad's old Rugby mates! We tried not to talk about it again.

Outside of Rugby work was going well and I was soon being told I should be looking to move on from the role I was currently holding, but doing so would mean moving from the picturesque town of Newport to the idyllic haven that is Port Talbot. In terms of a commute from home to work the extra distance wasn't too much of an issue, however there was no way I was going to be able to travel the extra distance to get to training on a Thursday night. This was looking like it would be my last season with Frampton.

Being my last season with Frampton also meant it would probably be my last tour (though this was never going to be the case) so Simon and I decided we would give the people what they wanted (or the youngsters) and organise a tour to Newcastle. Personally I felt the tour was an anticlimax as there is nothing better than being on a proper coach journey a few hours up the road and having a night out where ever we end up.

Newcastle of course had its high points; one of the highest was when Gally, a young muscled bound freak of nature did "the lift" on me from Sound of Music. The theme for Newcastle was also superb. We all went dressed as though we were on safari with the tour slaves dressed as if they were safari animals. We looked the part and definitely gained some attention as a result of it. Though what will always stick out to me is when the Club Captain Maccy was reciting "the wonderful thing about tiggers" to his slave in order for him to remember it upon request.

However without the Old Gits coming to visit us for their one nighters and the tour party being split by two flights and a train journey, it just didn't have the same atmosphere. Plus, England got smashed by Ireland in a grand slam decider that weekend!

My time at Frampton was over, I had loved every minute of it but in order to keep playing Rugby and for it to be practical I had to start playing over the bridge, and to this day, Dad I am sorry.

In to the Cuckoo's nest

Working and living in Wales I had experienced my fair share of stick for being English and not playing for a Welsh club, and after playing senior Rugby for over 10 years for the same club I found myself in the same position as I was when I was 18. Who should I play for?

I could play for the closest club to my house, Penallta, where I knew a few people, and I would be able to walk home after a few pints. However they were flying high and I wasn't getting any younger, and only getting slower.

I could play for Nelson where my father in law had a few connections, but it was probably just out of walking distance so no real advantage there and they had a reputation for being an "old-school" valley team. I'm not sure being English would be a welcoming trait.

My other option was to play for Risca Cuckoo's. Risca was a club that had been recommended to me by my work mate Chris. Chris was the club treasurer and had been pestering me for a few months to go on down, as well as selling me the clubs weekly lottery ticket.

As I was travelling to Chris' house every day in order to travel to work it made sense to play for Risca, so come pre-season I was on my way down to play for the Cuckoo's. Risca ran two teams as well as a youth team though after a few pre-season sessions it was difficult to decipher who were the youth players and who were in the senior squad, everyone was so bloody young. Even those that looked old were young, naming no names! Either that or I hadn't realised how old I had suddenly become!

After a few sessions and getting into the meat of pre-season the fixtures were soon announced, and out of pure coincidence one of the fixtures was against Frampton! I couldn't have written this! It was to be a good old fashioned coach trip down to Frampton to play a pre-season have a few bonding beers and get ready for the season ahead.

I was asked in the build up to the game if I wanted to play but I was adamant that my first game for Risca could not be against a team I had been with for so long before hand, it just wouldn't be right! However I was more than up for a coach trip and a few beers!

The Saturday came and it was a gloriously sunny day as we all met in the Risca car park ready for a little journey over the bridge. We set off and from what I had seen in pre-season Risca was taking a strong side down to play Frampton. As we came off the M4 the coach driver was asking anyone on the coach if they knew where Frampton was, cue my moment to shine: I could have got us there with my eyes closed.

The game itself was a bit one sided in favour of Risca and I soon realised the standard of the club I had joined. These boys were playing good Rugby and competition in both the first team and the athletic would be fierce - something Frampton had never really had the luxury of.

After the game it was back in to the clubhouse that was so familiar and was great to see all my old team mates mixing in with what would be my new team mates. Frampton put on a good spread and then the festivities began.

Firstly, as it was my first away trip with Risca I was dressed up in a beautiful matching two-piece blouse and skirt with matching handbag. I personally thought I looked delightful.

Then up stepped Mike Weaver. Weaves gave me a great speech and presented me with a framed photo of myself in a Frampton jersey. It was a touching moment. The moment that followed however was not so touching: I was presented a dirty pint with a pickled egg in the bottom. The lads knew I hated pickled eggs! However I got it down and I was done, or so I thought.

It was then time for the Risca lads that were on their first away trip to have a couple of cheeky drinks, this time topped with scampi fries. I'm not sure if this was an attempt to make the drink more nutritious. The first one went down no problem, the second, not so well. Luckily I by no means disgraced myself in the drinking stakes; probably because I had ten years on most of the lads I was drinking against!

The evening carried on in great spirits with the drinking games in full flow. After a while the lads wanted to sample another of Frampton's watering holes and were asking me where we could go. Luckily for me the Globe, which was all of about 400 yards down the road, had a beer festival on with live music and the players were happy and more importantly so were the committee and the powers that be.

As the night ended we poured ourselves back on to the coach to head back home to Risca. Some of the younger lads went on in to Bristol itself but I had most definitely had enough. Gemma was waiting by the phone for me to let her know when to pick me up form my first Welsh Rugby away day safe in the knowledge that I would have been looked after. When Gemma did finally drive down Risca high street to pick me up what she encountered was me, in my matching skirt and blouse, with handbag, falling out of the late night pizza joint. I think this pretty much set the tone.

With the pre-season finished and the league about to start I was picked in the centre to play for the Athletic away at West Mon. Having always played in the first team at Frampton I was a little apprehensive about what the standard of Rugby would be playing in the Seconds but as this game and the following two seasons would prove I had nothing to worry about. The standard of opposition may not have always been as tough as we required but the style of Rugby that we were playing was free flowing and made for good watching, as my Dad and Granddad will profess. It also meant I would be scoring a few more tries in the following two years; something that had dried up whilst playing at Frampton. I blame the greedy forwards.

The Athletic was being captained for the second year by scrum half and fellow Englishman and therefore ally Matt Plews. Having someone to share the English abuse definitely made it easier.

West Mon was an odd place to go as we had to park and change about a five-minute walk from the pitch, and when we got there a burnt out car was on the side. To add to things the referee must have known God. I have never seen a man so old with Rugby boots on. How he was going to keep up with play I would never know. Though we do have to remember without people like him giving up his Saturdays no one would be playing.

We won the game against West Mon comfortably and I even managed to score a brace on my debut, not a bad start. The one thing I will remember most about the game is playing alongside a small young lad of 18 who wanted to take on the world, but first he wanted to take on the much bigger and older West Mon front row, second row and back row all at the same time. This was the first time I would see Pricey lose his temper, though it would definitely not be the last.

Unfortunately as was becoming the norm I found myself injured, this time my shoulder. I couldn't move it above 90 degrees. Another few weeks on the sideline! Brilliant! Age really was creeping up on me, though not so much creeping more just jumping out in front and saying "ave that you old g*t".

I was only on the sideline for a few weeks, and during that time the Athletic had continued their 100% winning record but had picked up injuries in the firsts and second teams so they soon began to look a little different to what they did at the start of the season. This shuffling around also meant I was asked to play Fly Half. When I had been asked to play there for Frampton it was because I was the only option they had, being asked to play there for Risca was probably due to the fact of my age and being a bit more experienced than everyone else - not to do with ability.

The Athletic continued to march on, beating anyone that was put in front of them, and scoring heavily. In the first half of the season we were unbeatable. The second half of the season would prove much harder as we lost a number of fixtures to the weather. This was Wales and when it snowed, it snowed!

In Wales club teams are not allowed to play when their national team are also playing, which means there are weeks during the autumn Internationals that you don't play, and then again all through the Six Nations. To start with I thought this was a great thing as it meant I could go to the international games. Even as an Englishman a day in Cardiff on match day is brilliant - a lot like Disney without the Mouse. However after having two seasons in Wales it was a pain, it is a nightmare to fit in all of the league fixtures in the allotted time and you should be allocated as many weekends as possible. Even if this means the WRU enforcing morning kicks offs when the national team plays on the Saturday.

As any Rugby club will appreciate getting two or even three sides out every week takes a lot of effort, and is not made any easier when clubs pick and chose who they play. This may sound like me having a bit of a rant, and to a degree it probably is, but after having a very successful start to the season and travelling wherever we had to with a bare fifteen if needs be in order to get a game it was very disappointing to have a number of clubs cry off on the Saturday - some just hours before kickoff with all sorts of ridiculous claims. Personally I think it was because we gave them a tumping on their home pitch and they weren't willing to travel to Risca to play us at home. This didn't just happen once or twice but on countless weekends, and for two consecutive seasons and would have a huge bearing on us trying to win the league.

On one such occasion we travelled over to Abergavenny and produced a backs to the wall display to beat them. Again I was asked to play ten and kicked like a drain, but we dug deep and really did pull a victory out of nowhere. Then we were kicked in the teeth.

As with any other Saturday in the changing rooms someone asked if there was a valuables bag (a bag where everyone's phones, wallets, watches etc were collected) the bag was then usually locked in one of the player's cars to ensure the items wouldn't get stolen from the changing rooms during the match. This was the theory. In practice what we had actually done was collect everything valuable and put them in one convenient place for some little fuckers to steal.

Everyone was gutted, though some of us were extremely lucky, me included. For some reason I can't remember, I was going to be late to the game so I drove straight there and therefore kept all my valuables in my car. As a result still had all my valuables. As a point to note Abergavenny were one of the clubs who decided not to travel to Risca either season to play us.

The two coaches of the Athletic at the time were Richie Evans (forwards) and Adam Swithebank (backs). Richie was an ex first team number eight and captain who did not have a lot of time for other teams, in fact I'm pretty sure during every pre-match speech Richie would say "I fucking hate Abergavenny/Pill/Caldicot etc". It really didn't matter who we played, Richie did not like them.

Due to the number of games lost to international fixtures and the weather the coaches thought it was a good idea to arrange a friendly before the next league game - and we were to play Ebbw Vale on a Wednesday night. Ebbw Vale were in National League One and only lost out on promotion in a play off at the end of the previous season. If they were going to turn up with a strong side this was going to be a long night.

Without reliving all the details it was a long night. I have never played against a team that played at such pace for eighty minutes. I remember being in the defensive line and looking up to find someone to pick out, and there was no distinct difference between any of the forwards or backs-, they all looked the same. And not one of them looked like a traditional prop, someone like Zaff.

As with any club there are certain teams that you just don't want to play against. Playing at Frampton it was Southmead. For Risca it seemed to be Pill. Pill for those that aren't aware is a beautiful little hamlet situated in the picturesque town of Newport and I encourage anyone who is looking to go to Wales on holiday to pay a visit.

 I may be being a bit cynical but it wasn't the greatest of surprises to me when I was asked to play in the first team due to unavailability. My first team appearances did appear to be following a type of pattern that when we were playing against the less desirable teams players cried off and I was called up! To me it made no difference, mainly because I had never heard of these delightful areas and didn't know one place from the next!

My next call up for the first team was when they were playing away against Garndiffaith on a cold Saturday in December. Again for those that have never been to "the Garn" - and lets be honest why would you. The Garn was so far up the valley that it only ever has two seasons, winter and deep winter. It shares most of its similarities with Mordor. Including its inhabitants.

By this point the season back in England had finished and Frampton were preparing to go on their annual tour to Weymouth, when I heard that a space had become available I was not going to miss out. It would be odd going on tour with the boys having not played all season but I loved a tour and even though I would be a tour virgin having played for another club I was old enough and wise enough to know how it all worked and was sure that the younger boys would be getting most of the abuse - and thanks to Joe Ferris I was right. Joe had come through the youth system of the club and was a clown, a loveable clown, but a clown nonetheless. On your first tour the best advice I can give anyone is keep your head down, don't draw attention to yourself and do as you are told. Joe had quite obviously been given the opposite advice.

The tour was a good old-fashioned trip down to Weymouth. There was no game on the Friday and we just had a good day on the beers. I was sharing a room with my old masters from my first tour Badger and Shag Williams along with Slapper Tiley. Being from the old school of Rugby players I wouldn't have to do anything too hard, just ensure they had a cup of coffee each morning, wash them when they had a shower and make sure they always had a pint in their hand. Simple.

On the Saturday we set off to play our fixture. Due to the great numbers we had on the tour along with the Old Gits coming down to visit us for the day we had managed to get out two sides- a vets team and a first team. I was playing in the first team with a few lads I hadn't played with before but everything was still familiar; the moves were the same and I was back in the centre in a Frampton shirt, where I had been for many games beforehand. The game was played in great spirits and we threw the ball around looking to score from all areas of the pitch. Frampton ran out winners and I even managed to grab a try on my return to the shirt. For some reason it meant a bit more than a normal tour try.

After the game it was back in to proper tour mode and first was the naked run. Something that I would be participating in again. All I had to do was make sure I didn't come last and give a good showing. When I was twelve years younger this wasn't a problem, but now a days I had to worry. Lucky for me there were a few on their first tour that were either fatter or older than me, so not coming last wasn't an issue.

Back in the clubhouse our hosts were superb and we stayed there for quite a few hours with both clubs going through their repertoire of songs and Tony Slate leading the way as choirmaster. Being a slave meant that you had to be able to entertain the other members of the tour party and in recent years, thanks to Simon Cowell, we had decided to introduce Slave Idol on tour.

Slave Idol was very much like the TV equivalent in that you had three impartial judges who had questionable taste in fashion and a host that liked the sound of his own voice. The tour virgins were sent into a room to decide what they were going to bring to the party and then called out one by one to perform.

Being that I knew exactly what was coming up I had been preparing a couple of songs in the build up to tour. Fail to prepare, prepare to fail. The songs that I had been practicing were both by the Aussie legend Rolf Harris, with two little boys being my banker.

Tension in the green room among the slaves began to mount as one by one they were called out and maliciously mauled by the judges, even the sob stories couldn't save them. Then it was my turn, I was up, I knew I had practised enough to make my dream come true, this was my moment in the spotlight:

"Two little boys had two little toys...." I started softly instantly grabbing the attention of the crowd. I knew I was on to a

winner as it was Mike "Cowell" Weavers favourite song, and if I could break him the rest was a sure thing.

"Did you think I would leave you crying, when there's room on my horse for two..,"

At that moment I knew I nailed it, a tear trickled down Weavers face, there was a whimper from the crowd, and they were putty in my hands. I finished the song and accepted my applause. Surely all I had to do now was wait for the public votes to pour in and accept the trophy.

What happened next I can only describe as one of the biggest injustice since One Direction didn't win X Factor. As the results were called out I was only in second place! Second! Now I didn't mind coming second but this was a travesty of justice! I was pushed in to second place by singing asses, and that is not a slur on the slaves performing, they actually were singing asses! Since the results, there have been tabloid rumours that the only reason I didn't win was down to my Welsh connections, which was fair, so I moved on.

Touring back with Frampton was great; it makes you realise that your first club, no matter how great other clubs are after it, is the club where you will always feel at home and where your loyalty will lie.

While I was away the Athletic kept up their 100% winning record however due to other teams bottling it and not wanting to play us we were only in second place, although we did have 3 games in hand on the team that sat at the top. With the end of the season approaching we were desperate to get the final games of the season in, which coupled with also having to fit in a cup final and other teams not being very accommodating was proving very difficult.

The last three games of the season for the Athletic were two league games both against Pill and the cup final against Caldicot. These three games would decide whether the season had been a success, but even after not losing all season we could quite easily come away with no silverware.

The first game against Pill was our chance to win the league outright, even though we would have played 3 games less than our nearest rivals. All we needed was two points, whether that be a losing bonus point, a try scoring bonus point, or more simply we just needed a win.

The risk of playing teams at the end of the normal season in order to finish the league was that they would load their usual second team with first team players. On some occasions there are going to be first team players in with the seconds, when coming back from injury for example. But what turned up to play against us was basically Pill's first team. People say I might be making excuses for losing, but the fact I had played against Pill first team two weeks before it was pretty obvious. This coupled with the fact that Pill seconds had struggled all season and suddenly put thirty points on a team that were undefeated before this game stank of being stitched up! We also still needed the two points to win the league and had to go away to Pill. It was not looking good.

During the game I was also unfortunate enough to find my head underneath someone else's boot as they were rucking. During the game a bandage and a dollop of Vaseline stopped the bleeding but once the game was finished another trip to A&E was required. This time it was just a few stitches and with a bit of bandaging and I would be fine to play on the Wednesday. No dramas.

Before the Pill rematch we had a small matter of the cup final against Caldicot. We had beaten Caldicot twice in the league already this season and were obviously favourites going into the game. Everyone was up for the game and Richie Evans fired us up by telling us he "fucking hates Caldicot".

The game started brightly for us and we were soon a couple of tries to the good, playing our usual expansive Rugby. Jake Knapman (who my wife think belongs in a boy band because of his large hair) was playing Fly Half and was kicking like an absolute dream; the boy couldn't miss, and we didn't know it yet but it would be his kicking that would be the difference. By halftime the cup was as good as ours, though like every cup final there was always going to be a twist.

The second half we lost our way allowing Caldicot back in to the match with poor first up tackling and ill discipline and the longer the game went on the more we were at risk from letting the lead slip. There were only two minutes left and we were five points up but we were defending for our lives on our own try line. Caldicot launched one last attack and through a huge defensive effort we managed to push them out into touch and the cup was ours! Celebrations would have to wait as unfortunately winning a cup final on a Wednesday night when most people have work the next day doesn't allow for a big night.

The Saturday soon came around and everyone was up for exacting revenge against Pill and hopeful about picking up the points that were required to win the league. This was not going to be easy as last week had proven, and the fact that the Pill first team had finished their season also meant we would yet again not be facing their true second team.

Through this week there was a sense of urgency; I had never seen the boys so fired up for a game. The way we started showed it. Within ten minutes we were two tries up and by half time we had scored our third. Pill should not have got back in the game. We should have finished them off.

But come the second half Pill were on top; they had smelt weakness, their supporters were getting on our backs, and Pill capitalised on every mistake we made. Jake, unlike Wednesday couldn't buy a kick; we were in danger of losing the match and the league. Then it happened, Pill scored again and after kicking a penalty we were nine points behind with only minutes left. The league had gone… or so we thought.

With the last play of the game Pill were again attacking our try line but we were awarded a penalty for holding on. With no time left we tapped and went, quick hands across the line and the ball came to Ryan Dallimore, our Turkish waiter. Dally was like hot shit off a shovel and shot off up the wing, beating a few defenders before scoring in the corner. Cue the celebrations! Even though this wasn't going to win us the match it was going to win us the league; our fourth try and being within seven points meant we had a try and losing bonus point - the two that were required to win the league! What a finish to the season. What a season! League and cup winners!

As with any end of the season it meant two things, annual dinner and tour! Now I know I had already been on one tour, but that wasn't with Risca so this season I would be lucky enough to go on two tours – but unlucky enough to be a tour virgin on this one as well!

The annual dinner was first and unlike Frampton this was a gentleman only affair and would be held at the Rugby club - a good old fashioned do. My recollections of the annual dinner are vague which tells you the kind of night it was. International referee Nigel Owens was the guest speaker and had the boys in stitches telling stories about his career.

My wife picked me up from the club at 2 a.m. and a number of the boys were still going strong: so strong that when I woke up the following morning there was a photo on Facebook that showed there was still a handful there at 7 a.m. waiting for the breakfast cafe to open! Cracking effort. I however spent the rest of the day face down on my lawn with one of the worst hangovers I had had for a long time… another sign age was catching up on me, and fast.

The comparison in annual dinners at Frampton and Risca were stark. At Frampton everyone was invited, parents, girlfriends, wives and it was always held at a neutral venue and everyone paying for their ticket with their drink on top with Mike Weaver being the main speaker. Weaves always put a lot of effort in to his speech and the Plank award was always the highlight of the night.

Risca as mentioned was a more traditional event with gentleman only (apart from Amy the physio), none of the players or coaches had to pay for a ticket and very rarely a beer as the club stumped up the costs, usually thanks to some generous sponsors - and an outside speaker was always invited (paid) to entertain the boys.

Both events were equally as entertaining and both have their place as the amount of work that goes on behind the scenes by the WAGS of the club means it is only right that they should be thanked and invited to the end of season event, especially as they organise this as well! However with men being such simple creatures sometimes the club-house, other men, and a lot of beer is all they require. It raises the argument that two separate events is probably the only way to keep everyone happy.

It was a few weeks after the season had finished and it was time for the Risca boys to travel over the bridge, and embark on a weekend at Butlins, Minehead. Most of the boys were going down first thing Friday morning but due to work commitments I would be joining them a little later along with a Plewsy and the previous first team captain Moggsy. Driving both captains to tour did seem a bit like I was the club bitch and they were on a pedestal but this was definitely wasn't the case… well they weren't on a pedestal.

As expected when we arrived the boys were a little lubricated and we would be playing catch up. Risca's version of Mike Weaver was a lad by the name of Craig Thomas, or Kipper. Kipper was behind almost every stitch up at the club and when there was a social event or a money-raising scheme you knew he wouldn't be far from the scene. As we were getting ready to go out Kipper had the boys gathered around and dished out the punishments, obviously arriving late for tour was heinous crime, and this coupled with it being my first tour meant it wasn't long before I was just as pissed as the rest of them as we all headed out for a top night.

The Saturday, all the boys emerged with fuzzy heads and headed for breakfast knowing that the serious drinking was about to begin. The Wales and England national teams had embarked on their tour to the Southern hemisphere. Given the time differences this meant that the first kick off was 11am and therefore this meant that this was the time when everyone would be out and drinking from.

Before we all went out Kipper had a surprise for us all and handed out individual costumes, props and tasks depending on who we were. It was my worst nightmare: I was given a Welsh shirt and a welsh cowboy hat to wear for the day and my task was to sing the Welsh national anthem when the boys decided it was time. I was not alone, Plewsy my ally was also handed the same punishment. Singing the anthem was not a problem; both of us had been living here long enough to belt something out that sounded phonetically close enough. Wearing the shirt however was something I didn't enjoy.

This was not the first time I had worn the shirt of the 3 feathers; a few months previously my next-door neighbour and great mate Jamie Birkinshaw had passed away in a tragic motorcycle accident. Jamie was a top lad and one of the most enthusiastic Welsh Rugby fans there ever was. We both enjoyed great times during the internationals especially during the six nations where we were constantly ribbing each other.

At the funeral it was requested that everyone wear a Rugby shirt, and preferably a Welsh one. I was only too happy to oblige for him, and I knew as I wore it he was up there looking down laughing and pointing at me, and then at the funeral when the song "as long as we beat the English" was played I knew he was probably rolling around in stitches - but that was Jamie. I won't forget you mate.

The Saturday afternoon was great fun, as usual the Welsh had put up a good fight against a southern hemisphere team but they just couldn't find a way to win. The boys were in good spirits and the drinks were flowing. When it came round to the England game a number of the boys had found the pace a little too fast and had sloped back to the rooms for a powernap before we went out again in the evening. Unfortunately my ally Plewsy was one of those that went back, leaving me alone, to sing the Welsh anthem, while the English anthem was playing. Cheers lads.

The tour was great fun, though after a little swim on Sunday it was time for me to head home as I had to work on the Monday and couldn't stay the duration. I know it is incredibly poor form to not only turn up late for tour but to also leave tour early, but I do like to think I hit it hard when I was there.

Those that can, coach

They always say the second season is the toughest as people know what to expect but this didn't appear to be the case for the Athletic boys - we just carried on from where we left off, with a slight change in the coaching staff. Adam Swithebank who had coached the boys to two consecutive league titles had been offered a job, which meant he would not be able to commit the time to coach the boys and a new backs coach was required.

While I was sat in work my phone rang and it was Mr Risca, better known as Colin Wilks. Wilksy had a proposition for me. He asked me if I was interested in helping out Richie Evans in coaching the Athletic and looking after the back line. Having been with Risca a year I knew accepting the role would mean the majority of my work would come on a Saturday as the two first team coaches Ty Morris and Gareth Evans ran the sessions during the week.

After having a think about it I accepted, though I did wonder how they came to asking me, and by process of elimination I worked out that it was only me involved with the second team who had reached my peak and was not looking like starting a first team career. Still I was excited about the new challenge and thought if I wanted to have an excuse to come to the Rugby when I finally stopped playing, I should look to find one soon.

I signed up to do my level 1 WRU coaching badge, which wasn't so much learning about Rugby as anyone that had played the game for any length of time should know what they are talking about, but more about how to put your ideas and sessions across. On the level 1 course there was a mixed bag of abilities, from coaches who were coming towards the end of the playing career, a al moi, to coaches who had only ever picked up the ball once in school but their son was now seven and looking to start playing and their dad had been asked if he would like to do some coaching.

When starting out as a coach with no previous experience it was a great starter course and gave you a great deal to think about from how to progress drills to how to keep everyone involved.

When the boys found out I was becoming the new backs coach there was a bit of ribbing as to be expected but all of the boys were top lads and nothing really changed. The main challenge for me at the start was picking a back line for the match on a Saturday. Richie and me discussed things and agreed we would carry on with the mantra that those players that trained would get picked ahead of those players that didn't. It had worked so far and the two league titles and last years cup pointed to the old adage that" if ain't broke don't fix it".

Even though the coaching staff had changed, the results remained the same and we were still beating all comers and this time sitting top of the league with games in hand, surely nothing could stop us this year. Nothing apart from a new rule that was brought in stating that for a club to win the league they must play at least sixteen league fixtures. This is all well and good in principle but if no bugger would turn up to play us how can we play the fixtures! We were not the club that was calling fixtures off, we always made sure we got the two teams out there, even if it meant ringing everyone in the phone book on a Friday night and even on Saturday morning.

Away from the Rugby my job was becoming a bit stale and the glass ceilings were in place; I could see where I wanted to be but there were barriers in the way. Work was also becoming very frustrating as like Rugby you expect everyone in your team to pull their weight, especially the person that should be leading from the front. In work this was not the case as there were people who rested on their laurels and expected others to do all the graft. I think in the past I would have put up with it, but I was probably a bit too long in the tooth to stand for this anymore so rather than do the extra work I began to write a book. So I suppose without the boring job I wouldn't be doing this. However I couldn't carry on in the same job as when I become bored I become grouchy, and as my wife will confirm I am not fun to live with. So I started looking elsewhere.

At first I was looking in Wales though when Gem hinted that she wanted to move house as she wanted something bigger, coupled with the fact that she was meant to be based from Bristol, I was able to widen my job search.

It wasn't long before I was offered a role I couldn't turn down working for a well-known Bank on an exciting project, or as exciting a project can be when working in finance. I accepted the role and then gave Gem the nod to find a house. Like the previous house buying experience all the details like finding a house, putting an offer in etc were best left to Gem. I would only mess it up.

Sure enough Gem soon found a perfect house just outside of Frampton, had managed to rent out our house in Ystrad Mynach, and we were soon on our way to live with my parents for a few weeks until the sale could be completed. She really doesn't hang about does our Gem.

Back at Risca I was enjoying the coaching, mainly learning from Ty and Gareth, making notes after every session and helping where I could. This was mainly holding tackle bags as from February I was unable to play. I had managed to get a hernia whilst lifting plant pots moving house! In my defence it's a very big plant pot and one that could do a lot of damage if not lifted correctly.

The boyos were still sitting pretty at the top though with a few games of the season left and the first team ravaged by injuries we were now struggling for numbers and we had a tough away fixture against Monmouth on the Saturday. I had rung everyone I knew in Frampton with the offer of free beer but no one had come through. Saturday morning came and we still only had eleven, including a mate of Dan Ridleys (back row player) named Ed. Ed had trained with us once before and is the only person I know to turn up to a training session and when asked where he plays to answer "second row or full back". I have no idea how the two positions complement each other - even after all the coaching courses!

After a quick coaching conference with Richie I decided I would make the numbers up to twelve and play at Fly Half, just standing at ten and being a pivot, surely I could do that with a hernia. I then rang my sister in law Hannah's boyfriend Jon. Jon was in the army and was a big ginger lump.He said he used to play Rugby but it had been a while; however desperate times came for desperate measures. Jon reluctantly agreed to play and we were up to thirteen.

Thirteen would be a struggle but both Richie and I agreed we would prefer to play with thirteen than call the game off. On the way over to the game as Jon way playing I also had to convince Hannah not to let on to her sister that I was going to play. Reluctantly she agreed; good girl. Hannah is a teacher in Monmouth Comprehensive and mentioned that she knew quite a few Rugby players in Monmouth. She could see if anyone was available. Excellent, I phoned Richie and said we might make fifteen yet!

Hannah phoned around and sure enough managed to rope in one of her pupils, Harry. Harry reminded me of myself when I was his age, skinny and a little nervous about playing with the bigger boys. Also just as we were about to kick off Wayne one of our supporters agreed to don his boots at the age of 47 and help the boys out: we had done it we were up to fifteen which in itself was an achievement. However the game went was irrelevant.

Twenty minutes in to the game and we were three tries up, I couldn't believe what I was playing in - everything we did paid off. We had even scored from a cross-field kick and they never work! Sure enough with fifteen the boys began to tire though we dug deep and held on for what was the win of the season. Harry who looked like a scared school boy, probably because he was a scared school boy, played superbly and scored a hat trick, one try being pure class, taking the winger on the outside and scoring from inside his own half. I think it goes to show it doesn't matter who the coach is, as long as you have good back room staff around you, like a sister in law with contacts, you can pull a win out of nowhere.

Having just secured a new job and moving to Bristol this would be my last season playing and coaching for Risca. Apart from being Welsh which I know the boys can't help, they are all a top bunch and have made me feel really welcome.

The season ended with another league title and us just missing out on ending the season with a 100% record when we drew our last game, 5-5. Something to work on for next year when I have no doubt the boys will retain their league title. Also I want to wish Kipper the best of luck in his new role as Athletic backs coach - I'm sure he will do a great job.

Moving back to Bristol I will of course be back at the club where I started my Rugby adventure though this time in a player coach capacity taking control of the second team. I am just finishing my level 2 coaching badge and packing my bag ready to go on the Lions tour to watch the boys do us proud. So Warren if you do read this and want some fresh blood and new ideas, I'm available.

Appendices

Appendix 1 - Drinking Games

Universal drinking rules (all punishable by 2 fingers of your pint, unless otherwise stated)

1. Left handed drinking from half past the hour to the hour and then right handed drinking from the hour until half past.
2. No pointing
3. No swearing
4. No names
5. No dangerous pint – this means your pint must not be within a finger distance from the edge of the table
6. No saying the word MINE – penalty is ten press-ups.

Thumbmaster

This is an ongoing game that is continued throughout the day with no end. The game is introduced by the gamesmaster announcing that a game of thumbmaster has begun and nominating a thumbmaster.

At their discretion the thumbmaster will choose a moment when to place their thumb on the edge of something, this might be a table, a stall, a bar etc. When this is noticed everyone in the room who is believed to be playing must follow suit and must place the same thumb as the thumbmaster on the edge of something. The last person to do so will drink as a punishment and then subsequently become the thumbmaster.

Freezemaster

This is another game played throughout the day and has the
same rules as thumbmaster except you must freeze in a position
instead of placing your thumb on the edge of something. Again
the last person to do so will drink and then become the
Freezemaster.

21s

Everyone is sat in a circle and you have to try to ensure that
when you get to 21 it is not you that is saying it. However the
difficulty lies in actually getting to 21 without someone
messing up.

The game is started off by the games master by saying the
words "I would like to introduce a game of 21s to my
right/left" depending on which direction they would like the
game to start. They will then say either 1, 1 2 or 1,2,3.
If one number is said then the sequence of number continues
around the circle in the direction in which it came.
If two numbers are said i.e. 1,2 then the direction of the
sequence will change direction.
If three numbers are said i.e. 3,4,5 then the direction of the
sequence will stay the same but the person sat next to the
speaker will be missed out and the person next to them will
continue. All very simple.
If anyone makes a mistake, in terms of speaking out of term or
hesitating then they must drink two fingers.

Once the number 21 has been landed on, this may take a while,
then that person to start with must drink 2 fingers, but then they
must introduce a rule of their choosing. This can be anything
they want. For example they might want to do something

simple like substitute the number seven for apple, or make it a bit more challenging by saying that on every number that is divisible by 7 you should now stand up when saying it. Everyone else in the circle must abide by these rules, and again if they are broken 2 fingers must be consumed. The more times you land on 21 the more rules that you introduce, therefore the more complicated the game becomes, and the more drunk everyone becomes.

Whizz Boing Bounce

Participants sit in a circle and the game travels around the circle with each player making one of the following moves:

Whizz:

A whizz consists of pointing your whole hand, palm towards stomach, across your body. To whizz left, you use your right hand; to whizz right you use left hand, the next player must whizz in the same direction or use one of the other words.

Boing:

This consists of raising your fist at head height, with the inside of your arm facing the person who whizzed you. Boing changes direction. For example, the person on my right whizzes me, I raise my left arm and say "boing". The person to my right must then use their left hand to whizz to the person on the other side of them.

Bounce:

Consists of a boing action with both hands followed by a downward pull. Bounce skips one person in the direction the circle is travelling.

Whoever messes us or hesitates drinks.

Cantonese Whizz Boing Bounce

The rules are exactly the same as above but instead you replace the words whizz, boing and bounce with anything that sounds remotely Cantonese.

Bo Dereks Tits

A silly drinking game but a fun one: to start with a member of the circle will shout or say the word "BO" in the direction of another member of the circle, and that person will repeat the word "BO" back to the person that started it. The exchange of Bo's will go back and forth, usually in a variety of voices until one of them decides to change the point of attack and shouts "Dereks" in the direction of a new member of the circle, this person must react and shout "Tits" to another member of the circle. This member will then begin the sequence again my shouting "Bo" to a new member of the circle for the "Bo" tennis to begin again.

When this breaks down a drink is consumed.

Appendix 2 - Plank stories

The highlight of the Frampton annual dinner isn't the award given to the player of the season but the award that goes to the person who has managed to surpass themselves in terms of stupidity during the year. "The Plank".

As mentioned I had managed to win the Plank previously for my bag's French adventure.

As the name suggests, the Plank award is a plank of wood with a piece of rope through it so you can hang it round your neck for everyone to see who this year's village idiot is.

Here is a selection of some of winners from over the years.

Steve 'Edgy' Weaver- Breaking and Exiting

The first ever winner of this prestigious award. Edgy had got drunk in crossbow after a game; he ventured upstairs to use the toilet. Unfortunately, he fell asleep and awoke in the early hours of the morning. As he entered the bar area, the alarms sounded so he forced a window open and fled. Little did he know he had dropped his wallet and an hour later the police had surrounded his house. They arrested him and he spent a night in the cells waiting for the rugby club to provide a character reference.

Simon Brooks – Broken arm

The rugby club tour to Sidmouth brought around this classic. Simon drank himself into a stupor and was carried back to the hotel on the Friday night. Oblivious to anything, his arm was plastered by prop Paul Mayer as he slept. Simon awoke next day to be told he had tripped outside pub, broken his arm and had been taken to hospital to have it plastered. Simon played no rugby that weekend due to his 'injury' and his face was a picture when it was removed at court with a hammer by Paul on Sunday.

Mike Weaver – Pussy Love

Weaves two new kittens were annoying him as he packed his kitbag on Sat lunchtime. He decided to 'lock' them in the top drawer of the wardrobe but then forgot. Hours later as he entered the bar after the game he was told to ring home immediately. Jane was in tears as the kittens had apparently escaped through the bathroom window. Jane had spent 5 hours searching and knocking on neighbours' doors. As Weaves set off for home to help and console Jane, it all came back to him.

Dave 'Foggy' Fogden- Fishing incident

During an all night fishing trip, Dave was caught short and had to act quickly. He headed into the nearby undergrowth, removed his all in one waterproof suit and went about his business. On returning to his fishing spot, it began to rain so Dave put his hood up .Only to discover that in the darkness he had s*** in the hood of his waterproof suit.

Pete Zaffiro- Electric cat

The second fish related plank story involves another member of the front row brigade Zaff.

Zaff had recently put a pond in to his garden and decided that it needed some lights within the water that would be controlled by a switch within the house. Zaff considered himself quite a handy man and was confident he could sort the electrics himself.

After all the hard work on the pond Zaff was confident that he had done a good job and went inside to turn on the lights. Just as Zaff was hitting the switch to the lights in the pond a cat was feeling the heat and decided to take a drink of water from the pond. The switch was hit, the lights went on, and the cat shot thirty foot in the air.

Mark Smith- Soapy Breakfast

Smither and Weaves had gone away camping with their families for the weekend down to the South coast and after a few beers the previous night Smither was cooking his mate a fried breakfast, bacon sausage, beans, fried bread, the works.

They sat down to eat their breakfast and Smither was tucking in to his breakfast in the way that a prop usually does, he was shovelling it down at a rate of knots and before Weaves had even managed to pick up his cutlery Smither was mopping up his bean juice with his bread.

Weaves after tasting his breakfast asked Smither if he thought it "tasted funny", Smither replied saying that he really enjoyed it and hadn't noticed anything. Weaves tried again and said to Smither that there was definitely something not right and that the breakfast was a little "soapy".

With that Helen, Smither's Wife, walked in to the caravan and said in amazement "Mark, how did you manage to cook that breakfast we haven't got any oil?"

Mark replied saying "I used the little pot that was by the window".
"That was fairy liquid!"

So not only had Mark managed to substitute cooking oil with fairy liquid but had also managed to polish off his breakfast without it touching the sides and him noticing, a true prop!

Mark Chaplin- where's my fish?

Chaps had set up a new aquarium for his son. The next day some of the fish were missing so on close examination Chaps saw why. They were swimming behind the backing scene that Chaps had taped to the inside of the tank. Chaps still did not click that the backing scene should go on outside of tank and even returned to the shop enquiring about waterproof glue.

Mark Chaplin – mis-spelling

Chaps retained the title this year. On the lions trip to South Africa, Chaps had the job to sort the union jack flag with Frampton stitched on it , ready for the TV. Once in Johannesburg, Chaps proudly revealed the flag in all its glory to Deano, Weaves, Smither and Starfish. Something was not quite right.. it had been misspelt as FRAMPTON COTTERRELL R.F.C !!

Paul 'Charlie' Chaplin – where my Grandson?

Charlies son Mark was away with work and his wife was poorly so Charlie was asked to pick the youngest grandson, James, up from school. Off Charlie went nice and early and waited outside the school. 30 minutes had gone and all the children seemed to have left, but no James. Charlie, somewhat concerned, went into reception and the school were somewhat worried with the situation of a lost child. They ran James name through the computer but could only find a Lauren Chaplin.

''that's his sister '' cried Charlie but then it suddenly dawned on him that James did not go to the Ridings and he should of picked him up at the Frampton C of E primary school .

Mike West (Wasper) – Where is my caravan?

As mentioned previously Frampton had embarked on Weymouth for their annual tour. Instead of joining the rest of the tour party in the accommodation that had been booked for everyone there was a renegade group who decided to stay in Nathan Coles static caravan which was conveniently located just outside of the city centre.

During the night out in Weymouth as Wasper became separated from his caravan friends and was enjoying the nightlife with other members of the touring party and as is par for the course on tour became a little worse for wear. After the obligatory kebab it was time for Wasper to grab a cab and head back to the caravan.

"Where are you heading to mate?" asked the cabby.
"Caravan park" slurred Wasper.
Now as you can imagine Weymouth has more than one caravan park and as knowledgeable as the cab driver was, he was going to need more information.
After racking his brains Wasper remembered a few more details. "It's up a hill, and by the sea.
Again the description "by the sea" probably wasn't the most useful piece of information with Weymouth being a coastal

town however the hill gave the cabby something to work with so off he set and finally pulled up outside a camp site. Wasper was delighted so paid the cabby and got out the taxi.

After walking around the campsite it dawned on Wasper that this in fact was not the right site, unfortunately for Wasper he was now outside the town centre and taxis were not so plentiful. So off he set in search of his Caravan and a warm bed.

This particular night in Weymouth the rain was lashing down and the wind was blowing hard, it was definitely not a night to have to wander round the streets of Weymouth to try to find a caravan.

Three hours later and about quite a few miles under his belt Wasper finally found the caravan he had been looking for. He was welcomed at the door by Nathan who has described the site that stood in front of him as a rain drenched angry yeti. Wasper was not a happy bunny.

Appendix 3 – More tours

Plymouth

Plymouth was the first tour I was tasked to organise after being handed the baton by Weaves. I was determined to do a good job so I thought I would start off with a location that was easily reachable by coach but somewhere that was large enough for all the boys to have a good night out.

The coach was organised using the same company and driver (Bomber) that we had used in previous years. Bomber was a star and turned a blind eye to a number of things that many drivers would have had a nervous breakdown if they were to see.

The fixture for the Saturday day was confirmed after ringing a number of clubs in the area, all I had find now was the accommodation. As you can imagine not all hotel or B&B owners are ecstatic with idea of hosting a Rugby tour, even if we are usually the best behaved group that tours. Much better than the Bingo tours we had encountered!
After much searching I had secured the hotel, and thought I had struck gold. At twelve pounds a night per person, this type of saving meant there would be much more in the kitty for beer (a much higher priority).

We pulled up outside the hotel and on second inspection I think it was a spelling mistake online - it should have been spelt hovel. In terms of location we were in spitting distance of the town centre, however this was also the location that the ladies of the night liked to frequent - not ideal!

Upon entering the accommodation we were shown around and to our dorms. In some dorms there would be eight people sharing. Eight people sharing in normal circumstances would not be too bad, however we were not normal sized people and after a rough calculation it was thought that one room of eight people totalled a combined weight of 130 stone. The rooms were also arranged in to 4 sets of bunk beds, and it is no exaggeration when I say there was no room to walk between the beds, unless you turned sideways, and for some even this was a struggle!

Needless to say I received a bit of stick for my accommodation choice and in hindsight for the extra £20 a person a Travelodge may not have been a bad idea! Though in future years when the accommodation was slightly below par I could always refer them back to Plymouth and point out it was a step up.

Apart from the accommodation it was another successful tour, with the theme being Cub Scouts, and all tour virgins being dressed as Brownies. One of the highlights was definitely when we asked the Brownies to entertain us by doing a workout routine on the grass roundabout outside the Wetherspoons. A surreal sight.

Blackpool

The Las Vegas of the North, Blackpool, in my eyes is the ideal location for a Rugby Tour. There are no heirs or graces and everyone out in Blackpool is out for exactly the same reason - to have a beer and have a laugh. There is plenty of accommodation, all hosts are willing to take your booking, and not just take your booking but be extremely accommodating when you get there.

When I made the booking in Blackpool at "The Residence" I asked the owner what time the bar would stay open until. His response could not have been better. "If you are drinking, I'll be serving". Perfect.

The overriding memory of Blackpool was the behaviour of one of the tour members who shall remain nameless but does answer to the name "R Scott". Ok so he won't remain nameless. Some people may say that R Scott is misunderstood, but that weekend he was a nightmare. Though as much of a pain as he was, he continued to take all of his punishments and for some reason kept coming back for more.

It was also an expensive tour for R Scott. As explained before the tour, virgins are auctioned off and as the rules of an auction state you should only speak or move if you are intending to buy someone. Unfortunately for R Scott he failed to grasp this simple rule and Scott and his consortium ended up with all four slaves, which in order to not be charged for Greed in Kangaroo Court he had to then sell back to the club at a knock down price.

Appendix 4 – Acknowledgements

My first and biggest thank you goes to my Dad and Granddad for coming to watch me, no matter where I was playing, whatever the weather was like and no matter how bad the Rugby was, because lets be fair sometimes all three were shit. Without you both watching me week in week out, playing wouldn't be as enjoyable, plus I know if I didn't play it means you would be stuck in the house with Mum and Grandma respectively so I suppose looking at it that way I am actually doing you a favour!

Another huge thank you goes to my Wife Gem. Gem like my Dad and Granddad and has braved the conditions on a Saturday afternoon to watch me play, but that is not why I'm thanking her. I'm thanking her for not moaning when I tell her I'm going on tour, for never asking "are you sure you need that extra pint?" when I'm at the club, and for picking me up whatever the time, wherever the location and again whatever state I find myself in.

A special mention must also go to the Coaches who have helped me over the years to become a better player and ensure first and foremost that I enjoyed the game, these include: Steve Capon, Mike Weaver, Paul Beet, Liam Smye, Tony Slate, Lee Ashford, Reggie, Chalky Meek, Ty Morris, Gareth Evans, Richie Evans and again Dad.

There are a few specific people of Frampton I would like to thank for "looking after me" when I was a new lad to the club and to those that have become top mates over the years; Tony Williams (Shag), David of the Cornwall (Cornish), Badger, Mike Weaver, Pete Zaffiro and Nathan Cole.

Last and by no means least I would also like to thank all members of Frampton Cottrell and Risca Rugby Club as you all contributed to writing this book and making the clubs great to be involved in.

Me (on the left) in my younger days, the front row was looking likely.

The game I scored my first try for Frampton against Old Cryptians

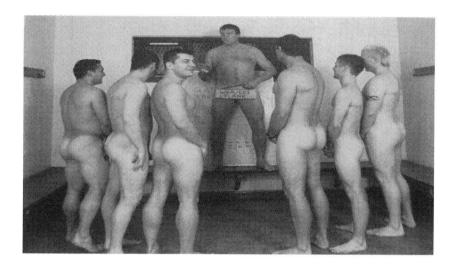

Weaves holding court

David of the Cornwall and Myself

7s winning side (Br: S. Belsten, Shandy, Mark Kane, J. Tiley, Me, Deano. *Fr*: R. Sparey, Shag, Rocco, A. Giles)

In full flow against Bishopston with imperious Keith Weaver (scrum hat, and Shandy in the background)

Celebrating after the win in the cup final against Old C's

Reggies promotion team after stuffing Chipping Sodbury

Attempting to play Fly Half

Plymouth tour – Cubs and Brownies enjoying a beer

Oooosh! Matt Lawrence can only look on at the brutality.

Tenby Country Gents on tour (L:R Maccy, T. Phillips, Shag, Me and J. Bennett)

The strangest thing to ever appear on tour. Jon Britton as a Homicidal, prostitute sheep!

My last season at Frampton before the Welsh adventure.

Try time at Risca.

Another try in the valleys.

Printed in Great Britain
by Amazon